A **Mail&Guardian** book

Mail&Guardian
BEDSIDE BOOK
2001

Edited by
David Macfarlane

M&G

ISBN 0-9584340-9-3

First published in 2001
by **M&G Books**
a division of M&G Media
7 Quince Road
Milpark
2092

Cover design by **Disturbance**
2nd Floor
101 Innes Road
Morningside
Durban
4001
e-mail: disturb@mweb.co.za

Page design by **Shaun de Waal**

Printed by **Formeset Printers**
22/23 Kinghall Ave
Eppindust
Cape Town
7640

Contents

Foreword

Howard Barrell

The first rule of newspapers is that a journalist should never forget his or her sense of superficiality. Or so we were told by Lord Northcliff, one of the British press barons in the early 20th century. It is, I am pleased to say, an instruction *Mail & Guardian* journalists do their best to disregard.

From what we know of Northcliff's concerns — he made a great deal of money — we can presume to know the assumption that underlay his statement. It was probably this: that sufficient human beings and advertisers (who are not necessarily the same species) will pay a newspaper a commercial fee only if its pages are unsullied by an indecent dose of what we are content to call reality.

In this, Northcliff may be right. But, in tracking the *Mail & Guardian*'s progress over the past two years — 30% circulation growth in a declining newspaper market — it is precisely our determination to forget our sense of superficiality that has attracted new readers to our pages.

This, of course, says something about our readers. It does not tell us that six out of every 10 readers are black, one is coloured or Asian, and three are white — though they are. Nor does it indicate that our readers are drawn from all classes — though that, too, is true. Neither does it necessarily follow that our readers are often well-educated and high-earners — though they are.

What our sales figures do tell us, however, is that intelligent people are seeking the newspaper out. They tell us that the *Mail & Guardian*'s distinguishing feature is the intelligence of its readers: the *Bedside Book*'s inclusion once again of readers' letters and *Notes & Queries* bears powerful witness to this. And that is an enviable state of affairs in which to be publishing a newspaper. Ask any editor.

Over the course of the past year, this characteristic of our readers meant, among other things, that in our coverage of the most important development — the terrorist atrocities in New York and Washington on September 11 — we could turn our attention quickly to the underlying issues. It was difficult in the pain and anger that followed these outrages to warn Americans that their future security might depend more on the United States's ability to be a good neighbour than a good warrior. But David Le Page and Drew Forrest, whose contributions open this selection, managed to do so with sensitivity and eloquence.

In "Colour me yellow", Thuli Nhlapo takes the reader back down the depressing dust-bowl road of South Africa's recent past in search of her family roots, and discovers a white lie. Sipho Madini's tale ("Found: Mr Madini") is another strange, choking tale of South African Anyman. It opens: "If you read *Finding Mr Madini*, or even if you didn't, maybe the reviews caught you. I am Mr Madini, the guy who went missing. One Sunday I was drunk and ..."

David Beresford, afflicted by advanced Parkinson's disease, wonders in "Is South Africa brain dead?" at the insensate response of South Africans to the news that one Bheki Jacobs (alias Hassan Solomons, alias King Solomon Solomons, alias Vladimir Illich Solomons) succeeded in passing himself off as a secret agent and in "reporting directly to the president" for five years.

Susan Leclerc-Madlala ("All that glitters, tingles and titillates") argues that one way of understanding HIV/Aids in Africa might be to view it primarily as a problem of men with money and women without. There is, she says, "a growing predation of young girls and women by older men". Mercedes Sayagues, exuberant exponent of anal sex in years past, discovers ("No pecs, no sex") the erogenous zone for the new millennium. And Cosmas Desmond delivers an excruciating, bitterly ironical assault on the decision by South African Catholic bishops not to relax their prohibition on the use of condoms to help prevent the spread of HIV/Aids.

Themba ka Mathe ("Anything goes ...") writes a picture of poet and performer Kgafela oa Magogodi that makes others appear depressingly boring and limited by comparison. Antjie Krog ("The writing of desire") provides a rare, well-informed insight into her fellow writer André Brink and his latest offering. Robert Kirby shows again ("The presidency disappears up its own fundament") that, when it comes to relieving us of the burden of our own or another's idiocies, the cut of his wit is as quick as any. His view of the Mbeki presidency is withering. And John Matshikiza's generous and relaxed voice, well known to readers of his weekly column in the *Mail & Guardian*, takes prose about as close to poetry as is possible on a newsprint page.

And much, much more.

Apart from seeking to be an organ of debate for our readers, we on the *Mail & Guardian* have also tried to deepen our own internal culture of discussion and argument. One way we have sought to do so is to encourage all staff to contribute towards the formulation of the newspaper's point of view. In our case, the editor is the final arbiter of this opinion. Elsewhere, developing a newspaper's viewpoint is the exclusive preserve of the editor and one or two others alone.

We have achieved a surprising degree of unanimity in the course of our weekly debates to decide the paper's view. Never was that unanimity more important than in the sentiments expressed in the editorial "A disastrous reign", which examined the presidency following allegations of an anti-Mbeki plot being brewed by Cyril Ramaphosa, Mathews Phosa and Tokyo Sexwale. Seriously perturbed at the president's behaviour on a number of key issues before the country, we asked in that leader: Is Mbeki fit to rule? No doubt it is a question to which we will return in the months and years ahead — and it is one on which we may well one day offer an answer.

Asking that question, however, endeared us to few in the uppermost levels of government — as we anticipated. It was, however, not their friendship or favour that we sought in raising the issue. Rather, as always, there is only one judgement to which we readily submit. And that is to the judgements of the perversely critical, difficult to please, irascible, unpredictable and intelligent species called *Mail & Guardian* readers.

There are few on the newspaper better equipped to talk to the idiosyncrasies of our readers than the editor of this year's *Bedside Book,* David Macfarlane, a man possessed of many of the same qualities. Who would have us any other way?

October 2001

How to make friends, not terrorists

David Le Page

T he rhetoric of war arrived within minutes, though war of any kind is unlikely to make Americans much safer. "We will hunt down and punish those responsible," said United States President George Bush shortly after Tuesday's attacks on the World Trade Centre and the Pentagon. The US media turned quickly to the military for its soundbites, which obliged reflexively, if sometimes uncertainly, with the rhetoric of counterattack and revenge.

It is probably not churlish to suggest that in the death and oblivion that has engulfed lower Manhattan many of those defence apparatchiks who watched miserably as their budgets withered during the Clinton years must see a chance for their interests to prevail again. In the short term their preferred responses to terrorism will certainly prevail, though these responses will not suffice. The formidable resources of the US — of the West and many other nations — will be directed at first to discovering and then punishing, by means fair and foul, those who planned the attacks.

Having somehow inspired martyrs to drag whole planefuls of souls into oblivion, those who planned the acts of terrorism are likely themselves to quickly meet death or justice. They are unlikely, however, to be praised as martyrs — even hardened haters of the US will provide little of the required sympathy. Not even the so-called rogue nations will resist the wrath of the world's most powerful country riding a wave of understandable self-righteousness — the speed with which Afghanistan's Taliban rulers leaped to distance themselves from the attack demonstrated how quickly realpolitik can inject a respectable facsimile of condemnation into hardened thugs.

In fact, Bush, the US military and the outraged politicians of the West are correct. The US must eliminate its enemies, must aim to wipe them totally from the face of the Earth. But to do so will require a strategy that it is probably far from willing to accept, or even able to consider. It is not a military strategy. It will not be based on building new clusters of anti-ballistic missiles, other innovative weaponry or unprecedented surveillance and intelligence gathering (the last an inevitable threat to civil liberties in democracies).

Rather, if it is to eliminate its enemies, the US must cease to inspire them. The sins of the US over the past half-century have been many, and the suffering it has caused very great. From Vietnam and sponsored killings in Nicaragua to militarily unjustifiable missile attacks against targets in Sudan (in response to the 1998 bombings of US embassies), there is no shortage of perfectly good reasons to hate it, if one is looking for such reasons.

This is not to say that the US is uniquely evil. There are few, if any, other nations in the world that conduct themselves much differently within their own spheres of influence. The US simply happens to have the greatest power to pursue its selfishness, and displays a certain lack of self-consciousness in doing so. How, now, can this wounded behemoth take the steam from the sails of those busy indoctrinating fanatical killers in remote corners of isolated nations?

The US must revolutionise its relations with much of the world. In the Middle East it must show as much intolerance for the excesses of Israel as it currently reserves for those of Palestinians. It must seek fair-trade policies with developing nations, pay its United Nations dues and show visibly greater respect for the opinions of the community of nations. Its foreign policy must demonstrate true respect for human rights, rather than their cynical use as a bargaining chip to be deployed against the weak and waived for the strong. It needs domestic policies — abolishing the death penalty and reducing its prison population — that demonstrate compassion, and not brutality, when handling its own citizens. It must take responsibility for its contributions to the global destruction of the environment and sign the Kyoto Treaty.

Some will argue that these are hopelessly idealistic or even irrelevant suggestions. But they will all work in different ways to end the conditions that make people ready to be recruited as terrorists, or ready to turn a blind eye to their work. The unemployment resulting from fairer or more principled trade would be a small price to pay for greater security, as would the costs of working to reduce pollution.

Certainly, these measures would never eliminate the need for a competent, unflinching military. They will take decades, perhaps lifetimes, to bear full fruit. But they could reduce, dramatically, the need to deploy the machinery of death against those whom the world has alienated somehow to the point of seeing their own lives as disposable.

Being a very good neighbour to the global community is the strategy that the US must somehow find its way to embracing if its citizens are ever again to feel truly secure in the world and in their own country. It is, unfortunately, the policy it is least likely to pursue.

September 14 2001

Against jingoism

I have been reading your paper online during this terrible crisis and have been very impressed with your coverage and with the general frame of mind your paper reflects. Here in Canada it is hard to find anything other than propaganda. Our papers are full of United States jingoism and hype, and our little social democratic party — the NDP — that has had the gall to urge restraint and reason is attacked daily. Keep up the good work: the world needs a multitude of views and particularly those of the less-affluent world. — *John Richmond, Canada; September 28 2001*

You are scum

I am a South African living in New York. Thanks to the utter crap you have written, and the truly disturbing views your paper has espoused, I will no longer read your paper and will do my best to ensure that those I know don't either. You are the worst kind of scum — you revel in the misery of others. Good night and good riddance. — *Chris Gerber; September 28 2001*

The two souls of the United States

Drew Forrest

"The tempest bursting from the waste of time
On the world's fairest hope linked to man's foulest crime"

The lines, by American writer Herman Melville, capture the complex nature of the United States far more accurately than some of the crude anti-US rhetoric sparked by the terror attacks two weeks ago.

It is not the Great Satan of radical Islamic demonology. It is the most brilliantly creative and energetic civilisation the world has produced, and its effect on every human being — including the world's Muslims — has been profound.

Anyone who has driven a motor car, flown in a jetliner, used a telephone or electric lamp, watched a film or listened to a compact disc owes a debt of gratitude to the US, because Americans invented the device, played a critical role in developing it or mass-produced it for the first time.

The US's impact on popular culture has been immeasurable, in part because of its unique multi-ethnic chemistry. Its music, rooted in African and British folk traditions, is the nearest thing there is to a global idiom.

The enormous productive power of modern industry is the US's prime gift to the world. It has been the difference between the politico-economic entropy of Europe in the 1920s and the socially integrated Europe of today. Its markets, which consume 40% of the world's resources, have been central to the great forward leaps of Japan, the Pacific Rim and, most recently, India.

Underlying its strength and resourcefulness is a Promethean vision of individual human beings as equal to any challenge, unfettered by the past and unafraid of the future. Despite the size of its underclass and the power of its private corporations, it remains a society that encourages individuals to invent themselves.

Much the same applies to the US's popular democracy. Sceptical foreigners point to the empty glitz of presidential elections, where campaign funding and marketing techniques seem paramount, and the absence of a meaningful multiparty system. But most Americans feel they own their government, and identify passionately with the flag, the anthem and the presidency, as supra-political symbols of nationhood. Significantly, there has never been a revolutionary threat to the US state. The underlying unity of Americans of all classes, inexplicable to Marxists, flows from the deep-rooted Puritan ideas of self-reliance, self-improvement and the equality of believers.

But there is another, darker legacy of the founding fathers that does much to explain the US's troubled relationship with the outside world. It is the idea that the world is divided between God's chosen and the spiritually lost, and that material success is a mark of God's favour. As in South Africa, Puritanism was the ideological underpinning of the destruction of indigenous peoples.

It was an idea given eloquent expression after the Washington and New York atrocities, when one US politician declared, "We were attacked because we are good."

Most Americans seem genuinely bewildered by the events of September 11. They can only explain such suicidal depths of hatred by recourse to a theory of crazed and wicked individuals, drawn to snuff out the light. The theme of countless comic books and movies, the opposition between super-heroes and super-villains is deeply engrained in the American soul.

It is an archetype that has surfaced in the tunnel-vision focus on

Osama bin Laden. Judging by videotaped interviews, Bin Laden is a heartless ideologue in the Pol Pot mould who applauds terror and considers American civilians legitimate targets. He appears to have provided military training and may have funded terrorism.

But not a shred of evidence has linked him to this particular outrage. His physical circumstances raise troubling doubts about the theory that he masterminded the attacks. Based in the wilds of Afghanistan, half the globe away from New York, he communicates face-to-face only. His vast wealth would have been irrelevant to a low-rent operation requiring pilots' lessons, airfares and a few Stanley knives.

A sick man with a kidney complaint who walks with a stick, Bin Laden may in fact have inflated his own role in the loose-knit international terror campaign against the US. Pakistani journalist Rahimullah Yusuf Zai, who has interviewed him and knows Afghan politics better than almost anyone else, believes he is driven by the desire to go down in history as an Islamic hero.

The complexities of Afghan politics and society also seem to be lost on the US. It is assumed that the Taliban's refusal to surrender Bin Laden is rooted in terrorist sympathies. Rahimullah argues that Taliban leaders have twice tried to prevail on him to leave, but feel reluctantly bound by his role in the Afghan war against the Soviets, and Islamic — but more specifically Afghan — customs of hospitality.

Nineteenth-century French political theorist Alexis de Tocqueville observed that Americans lack a sense of tragedy. Their optimism and confidence is a key source of their strength. But they have little insight into the flawed nature of all human beings and human projects, and particularly of their own moral deficiencies. If they had, they might see the glaring hiatus between their democratic professions and their support for tyrants and "torture states" over many years. They might see that their anti-terrorism stance seems hollow to many, given past US support for terrorism in Angola, Nicaragua and El Salvador. They might be more alive to the outrage felt by all Muslims over Israel's systematic abuses in the occupied territories, and perceptions that the US is indulging the Israelis.

Americans are a great people, and their economic power, vitality and libertarian traditions have a potentially huge role in making the world a better place to live in. But large questions have been raised by the US government's approach to the Cold War and response to terrorism. Does it have the spiritual and moral vision to provide the right kind of world leadership?

September 28 2001

The global revival of the left

Glenda Daniels and David Macfarlane

A groundswell movement for people-centred social justice is generating a momentum that amounts to the left's best hope for 30 years. It is a reinvention of the left that involves new formations in place of traditional communist parties and left-wing governments.

And it draws on a network of strategic affiliations among a wide range of new social forces and subcultural activities — including environmental groups, lesbian and gay activists, feminists, community-based organisations, anti-nuclear groups, non-mainstream media and alternative education. From November 1999 in Seattle to Davos, Bangkok, Cochabamba, Washington, Chiang Mai, Bombay, Buenos Aires, London, Istanbul, Lagos, Windsor, Johannesburg and Nice, powerful anti-globalisation demonstrations have targeted the World Bank, the International Monetary Fund (IMF) and the World Trade Organisation (WTO). And more are planned, right up to the Washington summit of the World Bank in October 2001.

But what is "the left"? As a socialist project deriving from 19th-century Europe, the left's raison d'etre was to realise the fullest potential of human beings, argues Eddie Webster, professor of sociology at Wits University. The 20th century saw this project taking form in three traditions: the communist, the social democratic and national liberation (as well as anti-colonial) struggles. "All three," says Webster, "have run their course now."

The new left activism includes historically oppressed racial groups, women, the self-employed and the informal sector — five-sixths of the world — that traditional left projects in effect excluded. These voices are now stronger than ever, and "the new left must take them as a starting point", suggests Webster. There is a global crisis of social disintegration, an increasing divide between rich and poor, rampant unemployment, environmental devastation and a lack of health care for the world's majority. All these result from what poet and activist Dennis Brutus has described as "systematic 'neo-liberal' injustice: market imperatives ruining ordinary people's lives".

The reinvented left is mounting a revolution against the neo-liberal dogma of governments, big business and mainstream media, which preach that there is no alternative to the supremacy of market forces. If we accept this mainstream version of reality, then the march of globalisation seems to be inevitable. We will also believe that widespread poverty, disease and unemployment can at best be alleviated, never eliminated. In other words, we will opt for fixing, not nixing, the system, or for reform rather than revolution.

But the "nixers", such as Brutus and other activists worldwide and in South Africa, are both calling for and coordinating new confrontations. These confrontations are challenging "large corporations, commodification of daily life, commercialisation of culture, destruction of indigenous livelihoods, intensification of patriarchy, fouling of the environment, and the construction of undemocratic, world-state institutions in Washington and Geneva", says Patrick Bond, professor at Wits University's School of Public and Development Management. Anti-globalisation demonstrations and protests are on the cusp of finding a programme to wage all these struggles cohesively, Bond suggests.

Yet the fact that these struggles rely so integrally on the new technologies (such as the Internet) that are part of globalised culture suggests that globalisation is more ambivalent than either its detractors or supporters assume. For instance, heightened communications technologies allow the new left to form an internationalist culture around human rights abuses.

Dismissals of this activism as loony-lefty raving are rendered problematic by the anxious seriousness with which police forces and the World Bank itself have responded, Bond observes. "When a hippie participant in a planning meeting for an impending demonstration inadvertently leaves behind a cellphone containing the chief of police's phone number, police infiltration can reasonably be suspected." And when World Bank president James Wulfensohn suggests that because the bank's meetings have become magnets for embarrassing demonstrations their dates and venues should be kept secret, we are clearly seeing something other than lefty looniness.

So is there a movement? Yes, says Bond, "it now adds up ... A common opposition to global apartheid and neo-liberalism now exists."

One strategy in this revolution is to hit the World Bank where it hurts most — the finances at its disposal. Eighty percent of these come from bonds it issues in return for funds invested in the bank. So: refuse to invest in the World Bank. Defund it, and so close it down. Nix it, don't fix it.

Sounds idealistic? Yet the city of San Francisco — the United States's second financial capital after New York — has kick-started a boycott of World Bank bonds. The city councils of Oakland and Berkeley have followed suit. This powerful start draws in a growing consensus of churches, unions, NGOs, municipalities and 40 US universities. One of South

Africa's premier universities, Wits University, now finds itself under pressure from within to join this boycott: it established a committee this year to convene a colloquium that will debate the issue.

This is emerging from a dismal context of a steadily eroding left vitality over the past three decades. Commitments to a human rights culture have been diluted through a neo-liberal surrender to the dogma that there is no alternative to market forces and to the belief that charity hand-outs constitute humanity's grandest strategy for dealing with poverty and other human suffering.

The reinvented left looks to diverse ways of realising human potential. Where earlier left traditions asserted the ownership of the factory or the state as the ultimate fulfilment, the new left promotes wider individual possibilities, for instance expressing your sexuality, your language or your "disability". "The new project," says Webster, "is to develop people's capacities."

Alarmingly, though, South African politicians are increasingly singing the global neo-liberal tune. President Thabo Mbeki often talks left but acts right; Minister of Finance Trevor Manuel and Minister of Trade and Industry Alec Erwin don't even bother to talk left anymore. The Reconstruction and Development Programme (RDP) was originally based on human rights demands (the same way the Freedom Charter was) but has been completely trashed in favour of the growth, employment and redistribution (Gear) strategy, with full World Bank and IMF approval.

Gear in practice involves the privatisation of water, for example. About 50 000 people in KwaZulu-Natal have been infected with cholera and more than 100 have died. This has followed Mbeki's reversal, following World Bank advice, of his promise of 6 000 litres of free water a month per household. Privatisation kills.

"New and intensified ideological attacks on the working class are the tear gas and Casspirs of today," says South African Communist Party secretary general Blade Nzimande. "Neo-liberalism's battering" results in "the job-loss bloodbath, outsourcing ... privatisation, and the rolling-back of the public sector", he says.

Trevor Ngwane, independent candidate in Pimville in December's municipal elections and head of the Anti-Privatisation Forum (formed last year), says: "I believe there is a revival of the left because of the dissatisfaction that is going on in the country, with the African National Congress having dumped the RDP, which was based on people's demands, to opt for the right-wing Gear policies, which were written up behind closed doors with the World Bank."

Despite standing as an independent, without party support structures,

Ngwane still polled one-third of the votes in his district. "The low turn-out at the elections is an indication of the lack of confidence people have in the government's economic policies. We need to consolidate into an organised left movement, and I believe we will develop this way."

Central to the new left is a renewed fight for women's rights. "About three years ago in the Western Cape, a new women's movement was organised, and around the country discussions and meetings are taking place exploring how to reignite the women's movement in South Africa," says Lisa Vetten, head of the gender research unit at the Centre for the Study of Violence and Reconciliation.

She points to initiatives in Latin America, such as feminist radio stations, newspapers and publishing presses. Attempts are also being made across Africa to link up activities and organisations around women's rights. Amanitare, for example, is an African partnership of organisations working in the area of women's and girls' sexual and reproductive health rights, as is Gender Links in Southern Africa. "Within developing countries generally, feminist thinking and action are also taking place in response to globalisation and its impact on gender relations, work, poverty and wealth," Vetten says.

Both in South Africa and internationally, all these on-the-ground movements have appeared for some time to lack coherence — in large part due to their hostile misrepresentation by the establishment in all its forms, including much of the media. But they are linking arms around the globe through subcultural activities, technology and shows of mass unity.

Labour, too, is contributing to the reinvention of the left. The Congress of South African Trade Unions's secretary general, Zwelinzima Vavi, says unions have to engage beyond narrow worker interests and have a voice in education, the homeless, environmental issues, the Aids crisis and women's issues to survive the new order. "We may not have a second chance for survival. We have to have alliances locally and internationally, and this is what's beginning to happen. Unions around the world are in the mood to confront neo-liberalism, the World Bank, the IMF and the WTO." Vavi says in the south a coordinated strategy has begun with the establishment of the South Initiative on Globalisation and Trade Union Rights, driven by Cosatu and Australian, Brazilian and South Korean unions.

These movements are all fighting to change a global political landscape that can appear unchallengeable. After all, just 15 years ago it was standard for the mainstream to refer to South African liberation activists as terrorists; now it's inconceivable that anyone would do so. Equally, current anti-globalisation activists who are demonised variously as anarchists, lunatics or pipe-dream idealists — who "don't know what they're talking about" (according to trade and industry minister Alec Erwin) — are humanity's best chance of surviving, and of creating a better world.

February 16 2001

The new left in a precarious present

Helena Sheehan

Reading "The global revival of the left" by Glenda Daniels and David Macfarlane, I thought: "This is where I came in." I was part of the 1960s "new left" who believed that we understood the world anew and would turn it upside down. We would push aside the old left with all its stodgy talk of the mode of production and the role of the state. We highlighted gender and race and culture and the relationship between the personal and the political in a way that the old left did not seem to do. We initiated a flourishing of new forms of political activity, a vibrant global counter-culture.

But we were also so myopic. We didn't really grasp the nature of political and economic power. Moreover, we didn't know as much about the old left as we thought we did. Those of us who stayed around when others were gone tried to understand why history moved on in a direction so disdainful of our desires. One insight of the early Students for a Democratic Society in the United States was the necessity "to name the system". When the energy of the new left began to dissipate, I decided to look to the old left, which was, I found, much better at naming the system.

This idea of a plurality of social movements replacing left parties has been around for several decades now. Empirically, of course, it is true that many inclined to the left have put their energies into these movements as opposed to left parties, but this is much of the problem of the left, not its solution.

Theoretically, I believe that activism in terms of race, gender and, let us not forget, class needs to be underpinned by naming the system in which an oppressive division of labour and an inequitable distribution of resources are rooted.

The older left named the system as capitalism and conceived of a systemic alternative to it: socialism. For Eddie Webster of Wits University to say that the oppressed five-sixths of the world has been excluded by the traditional left is obviously and outrageously false. The left has embraced all the oppressed of the Earth. It has brought light and literacy, health and hope to sections of the population in parts of the world that had known only unrelenting darkness, degradation and despair without it. It has addressed the exclusions of class and race and gender far more coherently and actively than any other force, because it has done so within the framework of an analysis of the nature of the social order.

The new movement is attempting to link the plurality of oppositional forces together at least at the level of strategic activity. It is also struggling to name the system. However, there is considerable confusion about doing so, with your authors adding to the confusion. Those who characterise the new movement as an anti-globalisation movement are failing to name the system accurately and to name its opposition appropriately.

Why should the left be against globalisation as such? The left is opposed to a particular version of globalisation, a globalisation dominated by the neo-liberal agenda, a globalisation that prioritises market forces above all other social ties. The left has always stood for an alternative globalisation and much of it is doing so within that tradition. To quote Blade Nzimande and Zwelinzima Vavi, as your authors do, in support of the critique of neo-liberalism and the aims of the new movement, without making the point that they do so in a way that is in conscious continuity with the older traditions of the left, is misleading.

Much of this new left is still the old left trying to find its way in new times. Your paper and your authors have taken this movement seriously and have not reduced it to a crowd of crazies who can travel with the same mobility as international financiers and clash with local police for their kicks. Behind those on the streets of Seattle and Prague are masses who cannot be there because they are poor or have jobs that keep them where they are, but want to be part of a force addressing and confronting the nature of the global system that defines their world.

To say that communist, social democratic and national liberation movements have run their course, especially here in South Africa, is not right. I have been involved in all three of these movements in past decades in the US and in Europe and there is no doubt that they have changed dramatically and drastically, but they have not left the stage. Here the African National Congress embodies in an unstable equilibrium all three traditions, as well as those who believe that there is no alternative to the neo-liberal agenda. These traditions are playing themselves out here in new ways, and time will tell what will be the outcome.

The growth, economic and redistribution strategy, for example, is perhaps most contested from within. People moved by these traditions did not lead difficult, dangerous lives for all these decades to make South Africa safe for bull markets or a cozy haven for knighted press barons to entertain the world's rich and famous and to leave masses hungry and homeless. The left has won state power here in a context in which enormous power resides elsewhere. It is traversing treacherous terrain.

The whole world is not only watching but pulling in different directions. Paradoxically, although the world is more and more tightly organised into a global system, there has been a decline in ability to think historically and systemically. It is necessary to get the story right, to name the system correctly and to build a movement accordingly. The left in this precarious present must find its continuity with its past in forging its future.

March 2 2001

NOTES & QUERIES

More than 200 years ago William Blake wrote a famous poem, "Tyger! Tyger! burning bright ..." In late 18th-century London, could Blake have ever seen a living, breathing tiger?
● He might have spotted a tiger, but I tell you what, he definitely wouldn't have seen a gorilla! That's why Blake never had the imagination to write about me. "Gorylla, Gorylla burning bright ..." — *Max's Gorilla Movement, Johannesburg zoo*

When I kill cockroaches using an aerosol spray, they invariably die belly-up. Why? Do other pests behave similarly?
● I have, after years of scientific research into the unnatural mortality of insect pests, discovered that striking a cockroach with almost any type of footwear has many advantages. It is more economic and environmentally friendly than insecticide sprays, and there is no accompanying unpleasant aroma. Moreover, a percussive instrument usually leads to a more immediate and hence kinder extinction. While demanding greater courage and an advanced degree of stealth on the part of the hunter, the prey invariably dies the right way up and hence with dignity. The great disadvantage with this method is that, on occasions, the reliquiae of the deceased become less intact, leading to more complex funerary rites, obsequies and procedures for the predator to perform. The post-mortem may also create a slightly uneasy feeling. — *Paul Wiseman, Rio de Janeiro, Brazil*

No money, no food, no one gives a damn

It is with utter disgust and dismay that I write this letter. The date for old-age pension payouts was today, February 6. Upon arrival at the various paypoints we were informed that there was no money available and that we will be receiving our payouts next week. The reason given for this is that the system is being modified. No one considered letting us know in advance about the change and the non-payment of pensions.

Maybe if you are sitting high up in government or just any other job you do not realise the total devastation caused by actions such as these. Let me attempt to describe it to you from a pensioner's point of view.

I was up very early this morning. I had my bath in record time; I had to get to the paypoint to collect my pittance. (Notice, no breakfast, the bread lasted only until yesterday, but no problem, today is payday and breakfast and lunch can be substantial.) I had R3 in my purse, just enough to get to Jeppe Street post office to collect my pension. My return fare was no problem; I was getting my pension. I got into the taxi. It was naturally full of oldies like myself, for it was pension day. Old Aunt Rosie next to me was just explaining to me that she had borrowed R3 from her neighbour to get to town.

It was such an exciting ride — we were getting paid. We arrived at the post office, and to our absolute horror we were informed that we would not be paid this week but only next week, as they were changing their system. This was done without consideration for us, no one considered it important to inform us, no one thought it necessary to put a contingency plan in place. We were given a toll-free number to call (0800 220 260), which just rings and rings all the time until you are forced to hang up. This situation is totally and utterly deplorable. It is unacceptable that this can happen with no one being held responsible or accountable.

I would like to emphasise the plight of some of us. More than half of us were stranded at the Jeppe Street Post Office without R3 to get back home. We now have a full week ahead with no money, no food, no money to pay the necessary bills. The worst part is that the culprits have not a care in this world. What is it about change and democracy that causes ordinary people to suffer in this way? What is it about democracy that makes one forget suffering and inequity?

A society that cannot look after its aged will be unable to look after much else. When will we stop suffering? We suffered before and were only given half what our white counterparts were given. Now we are left penniless for more than a week, by our own children whom we brought up with great hardship and the barest necessities. It is painful that today these are the very children who are pushing us aside and letting us suffer.

Someone needs to take responsibility. Someone needs to apologise and, more importantly, someone must ensure that this never happens again. — *Vesta Smith, pensioner, Noordgesig; February 16 2001*

About that 4x4 ...

It would be grossly unfair to simply assume that without spending a cent Tony Yengeni has been driving a luxury motor vehicle supplied by a successful arms deal tenderer. As everyone knows, some senior ANC representatives are prepared to pay handsomely for their driver's licences. — *Plus ça change, Sandton; March 30 2001*

Joe Slovo, thou should be living at this hour

The African National Congress's move from popular liberation movement to party of the black bourgeoisie has evidently reached a new plateau. The ANC is so secure in its new position that it can openly address some of the problems it is beginning to face as the party of the black rich.

There was a time when cadres were selflessly deployed by the ANC to serve only the interests of the ANC. This usually meant being deployed anywhere and in any capacity to serve the interests of the poor, above all others.

To be "deployed" today is evidently an assumed guarantee of lifelong privilege and status. It is this transformation which explains why the focus of the brouhaha over Tony Yengeni's R400 000 car has been on how he got it rather than that he is happy to be seen in it. Driving a status symbol that costs more than most South Africans earn in a lifetime proclaims that personal enrichment and esteem have become the ANC's new Freedom Charter.

At the time that ANC cadres began wearing suits, Joe Slovo warned of the "suit syndrome": those wearing suits usually ending up thinking and behaving like suit-wearers. The R1 000-plus suits Tony Yengeni is reputed to wear are each twice the monthly income his government provides pensioners. From suits to luxury cars is a small step. And from cars to helping senior ANC members make sure they will continue to have suits and cars even after they leave office is but a further small hop. Joe, thou should be living at this hour. — *S Ruben, Wynberg; April 6 2001*

Corruption scoreboard

Each week you produce another tantalising story of our rotten, corrupt society. Each week, new revelations about ministers or relatives thereof, civil servants at various levels, or plain political minions, are set out for our edification. The following week it is the turn of somebody else. This plethora of greed weighs us down. But there is often no follow-up. Can you please run a scoreboard of reported cases together with updates? I realise that this may need several pages in the saga of the 4x4 man, but others would be shorter. — *B Dixon; August 3 2001*

My bank tried to steal R25 from me!

This week I caught my bank red-handed trying to steal R25 from me. It came at the tail-end of a trail of the sorriest service I have yet received.

The bank — one of the big four — had been transferring an amount from my current account to a defunct credit-card account that I could not access. I wanted the money transferred back to my current account and stupidly believed this would be a simple matter, involving a simple phone call. A number of phone calls to my branch and to the bank's card division resulted in four promises to get back to me, none of which were kept. My branch manager was on sick leave, it transpired, and her replacement was out for the day. The person left in charge was out on lunch.

Eventually, someone at the card division ordered me to go to my branch with identification. Out of desperation I took some time off work to do this. I was made to wait in a little office for 40 minutes, at the place where I have banked for seven years, while the "problem" was sorted out. From here I could observe disturbing, chaotic scenes of barefoot clerks (I swear!) walking around dealing with vast sums of other people's money. From inside the main banking hall I heard a raised voice complaining bitterly, in Afrikaans, that this was the worst service he had received in his entire life. I shuddered.

At long last a clerk came to me and tried to coerce me into signing a withdrawal coupon. I had requested a transfer, but by that point I felt that taking the cold cash and running was probably the best option anyway. I was about to sign when I noticed that the amount was somewhat less than that due to me. I mentioned this to the clerk. "There's a R25 fee for cash withdrawals," she said. I said this seemed very high and, anyway, it was inappropriate as the mistake had not been mine. She left me irritably and returned after a couple of minutes with the missing R25 reinstated.

I counted my money carefully and fled. — *Horrified, Bezuidenhout Valley; May 18 2001*

Eat your sombrero, George W Bush

John Matshikiza

T he French have always run their colonies with so much more panache than the bumbling British.

So while the Brits continue to make a show of post-colonial regret (much of which is dedicated to the proposition that "we should have never abandoned our woggies to their fate, they just weren't ready") the French sail on upon their imperial mission unaffected by guilt, remorse or self-doubt.

And of course the Franco-Africans (or their leaders, at least) play along beautifully. There was, for example, that unforgettable moment when Emperor Bokassa of the short-lived Central African Empire arrived in Paris to attend the funeral of the late General Charles de Gaulle. As the emperor descended from his plane, he burst into tears and threw himself into the arms of French President Valery Giscard d'Estaing, wailing, *"Papa est mort! Papa est mort!* [Daddy is dead! Daddy is dead!]."

You couldn't imagine Jomo Kenyatta putting on the same kind of display in the arms of Queen Elizabeth at the funeral of Winston Churchill, could you? Us Commonwealth Darkies just don't behave like that. It isn't cricket. And besides, Her Majesty would have been seriously unamused.

The France-Africa summit in the Cameroonian capital of Yaounde two weeks ago was yet another display of the firm grip the French have on their erstwhile colonies. While the Cameroonian head of state Paul Biya was allowed to play the role of host, the agenda was clearly set by the chief among his guests: French President Jacques Chirac.

This 21st summit between French and African heads of state was billed as a celebration of "the eternal friendship" that was said to exist between the peoples of France and the Dark Continent. The bloodshed and brutality of the years of slavery and colonisation that had led to this somewhat one-sided bond of friendship were quietly kept off the agenda.

High up on the official agenda was the issue of globalisation, and what Africans were going to do about it. And it wasn't as if the Africans were being given much of a say in the matter, either. True, one African leader after another stepped up to the podium to throw in their small objections to the effect that globalisation was having on their already beleaguered economies.

But the bottom line was that globalisation was a reality, introduced from far away, like all the other realities that Africa has had to adjust to over the years, and there wasn't much the gathered heads of crumbling states could do about it-except maybe buy more Coca-Cola to help ease the pain. Cameroon, the host for this expensive and seemingly futile exercise in summit politicking, had already had to suffer the bitter pill of structural adjustment. The French president's opening eulogy to the country, paying homage to its culture, its noble history (Cameroon is one of the few African countries to have waged an armed struggle against its French colonisers) and its present "economic vitality", was evidence that Cameroon was seen to be playing the game.

And yet, in spite of some frantic efforts at a late stage to clean up the rotting streets of Yaounde and the commercial capital of Douala, the country's infrastructure shows few signs of vitality, or even direction. What economic vitality there might be is evidenced only in the bustling export of rich raw materials, and the crippling cost of having to import almost everything else. Health, education and other social programmes have been cut back so that the country can start to pay off its external debts. And naturally, the emotive issue of debt repayment to the West was another of those troublesome matters that was studiously kept off the official agenda.

The real coup pulled off by France was to have expanded its roster of "eternal African friends" beyond its former colonies. The Anglophones (including South Africa, Namibia and Zimbabwe) were also there this time, straining to decipher what crumbs the complex circumlocutions hidden in the formalities of the French language might hold in store for them.

But then came the announcement, almost before the real business of the summit had begun, of the probable assassination of Laurent Kabila, who had been due to show up at the summit on the second day. It was a moment that could almost have been stage-managed for effect.

Robert Mugabe immediately abandoned the conference to return to Harare, to be at the bedside of the ailing Congolese leader, who had supposedly been flown to the Zimbabwean capital for emergency treatment, but who was in fact already lying dead in Kinshasa. The other African delegates milled around in confusion, striving to comprehend what meaning this act of violence in the violent Congolese capital might have in the insignificant play of African politics.

Only Jacques Chirac remained calm, delivering, according to a commentator in the journal *Jeune Afrique*, a statement in which he joined in the fears of many of his brother presidents gathered at Yaounde, that certain unnamed African nations (not present at the summit) might have been behind this dastardly deed, hoping to destroy the integrity of that indecipherable entity called the Congo. And then, accompanied by a rousing farewell of truly folkloric Cameroonian drumming, the French leader boarded his plane and flew back to the real world, to get on with the business of dealing with more serious aspects of globalisation.

For sheer post-imperial aplomb, it was a performance that would have made George W Bush eat his sombrero, and Tony Blair barf into his bowler hat.

February 2 2001

The world's most dangerous rogue nation

Salim Vally and Patrick Bond

A quick and somewhat bloody "teach-in" on foreign policy was held at the Wits University Great Hall last Friday, in the form of a vibrant human rights protest. United States Secretary of State Colin Powell was forced to spend an extra hour hemmed in on campus by demonstrators, learning why the US is now widely regarded as the world's main rogue state.

Wits students engaged in non-violent civil disobedience and blocked the US delegation's exit. For their trouble, security forces roughed up students David Masondo and Nick Dieltens, who both received nasty facial and head wounds.

Throughout the day, members of Powell's security entourage patrolled the campus, on occasion ripping down posters critical of US foreign policy. A student was also "requested" to cover up his Che Guevara T-shirt because it was deemed "offensive".

This arrogance and coercion seems to have been the trend throughout Powell's tour of Africa. Aids activists in Kenya say they were prevented by US officials from unfurling a banner that read: "Put lives before profit." Nevertheless, in spite of Powell's militaristic buffer, the message got through: while he may have a respectful audience in Pretoria (and in banal *Sunday Times* coverage), he's more often considered, as a sign said, "The Butcher of Baghdad".

It was appropriate that the Bush administration's envoy received such an inhospitable welcome for several reasons. Firstly, Powell is personally responsible for an attempted cover-up of the horrific 1968 My Lai massacre of women and children by US forces in Vietnam; for participating in the mid-1980s cover-up of the Iran-contra arms scandal; and for covering up and downplaying 1991 "Gulf War syndrome" diseases and violations of the Geneva Convention associated with the mass slaughter of retreating Iraqi troops.

Secondly, Powell's responsibilities for human rights violations continue, through Washington's coddling of the apartheid state of Israel, which with US financial and military support is killing hundreds of Palestinians; the illegal blockade of Cuba, in the wake of at least 17 CIA assassination attempts on Fidel Castro; a $1,5-billion escalation of an alleged "drugs war" in Colombia, which in reality is merely another failing counterinsurgency in the tradition of Indochina, Central America and Southern Africa.

Thirdly, there are other features of the Bush administration's disregard for the rest of the planet's citizens that Powell should have answered for: the refusal to honour more than $1-billion in United Nations dues; the retreat from international efforts to curb illicit money laundering; the rejection of obligations to stop trashing the environment through the Kyoto Protocol on carbon dioxide emissions; massive military expenditure in the form of the "Star Wars" missile defence programme; a new attack by the US Office of the Trade Representative on Brazil's ability to produce anti-retroviral generic drugs to combat HIV/Aids; the recent refusal by Washington to fund organisations that provide family planning and abortion services in the Third World; sabotage of Korean peace talks; the nomination of men with appalling human rights records to the United Nations and Organisation of American States; insistence on Third World countries' repayment of illegitimate foreign debt to the World Bank and International Monetary Fund (IMF); ongoing demand that other countries adopt the World Bank and IMF free-market "structural adjustment", which cut the living standards of Africans while promoting transnational corporate and banking interests; and continuation of the extremist trade liberalisation process of the World Trade Organisation and African Growth and Opportunity Act, while hypocritically retaining protectionist tariffs at home.

No one should really be surprised at the aggressive record of the Bush regime in these vital areas, though, given its origins in a banana-republic election in Florida. Thanks to Governor Jeb Bush and five white Supreme Court judges, African-American voters were blatantly disenfranchised. Though Powell is black, he serves alongside people who have promoted apartheid and repression of Africans.

Vice-President Dick Cheney, for example, voted in favour of keeping Nelson Mandela in prison and against anti-apartheid sanctions in the US Congress during the 1980s. As the CEO of the oil services company Haliburton during the 1990s, Cheney sustained the Sani Abacha regime in Nigeria. And while the Middle East, Colombia and Cuba are just three current sites of US aggression, our region knows Washington's history of meddling all too well: the CIA's decades-long support of the apartheid regime; encouragement of Pretoria's invasion of Angola in 1975; US patronage of Renamo's war in Mozambique; Ronald Reagan's "constructive engagement" policy, which prolonged apartheid's life during the 1980s. During his term as president, Bill Clinton apologised to the people of Central America for the US's record of malign intervention, and Powell should have done the same while here.

The critique of US foreign policy may be loudest when students protest, but it behoves our Department of Foreign Affairs to consider why Washington's international illegitimacy was confirmed by the US's own peers in the UN. Over the past few weeks the US was stripped of its seats on the UN Human Rights Commission and the UN international drug monitoring board.

Human rights activists across the world celebrate the growing rejection of the world's most dangerous rogue nation, including its main foreign policy representative, Powell. Will a US delegation return to Johannesburg next September, at the Rio+10 Summit on Sustainable Development, for more evidence of international opposition to Washington's multifaceted war on the planet?

June 1 2001

NOTES & QUERIES

Do you qualify as a member of the mile-high club if you were on your own?

● Yes. The club takes all comers. — *Neil Hickson, Johannesburg*

● Of course not, you wanker. — *Brian McMillan, Johannesburg*

If you are in seventh heaven what did you experience in the first to the sixth?

● Exactly the same things as you did going from cloud one to cloud nine: your first bicycle; your first real kiss; the first time you made love; your first car; the second time you made love realising the first time was only half as much fun; the day you got your first job; the day your mother-in-law lost hers; the day you were selected for the Proteas; and the first time you smoked dagga (no offence, Herschelle, keep up the good work).

— *Robert de Neef, Howick*

Communists and social democracy

Tom Lodge

History shows us that communist parties can thrive in liberal social democracies. Before World War II, the most formidable communist party in Eastern Europe was in Czechoslovakia, a reflection of that country's level of industrialisation, strong trade unions and a relatively developed welfare state.

In freely contested elections in 1946, in the aftermath of German occupation and liberation by the Red Army, the Czech Communist Party won 38% of the votes, giving it a powerful presence in a coalition government. Here communists had genuine prospects of winning power through the ballot box as well as working-class, factory-based activism. Instead, though, a Stalinist leadership opted to use their control of the police and the Ministry of Interior to impose a tyrannical "people's democracy" in 1948.

More widely, post-war democratic Europe appeared to offer communists favourable opportunities for non-revolutionary progress to socialism. The French and Italian parties could build on the prestige accumulated through their heroic role in anti-Nazi resistance movements. Italian communists were to draw upon the intellectual legacy of Antonio Gramsci, who in the 1920s had argued in favour of a "war of position" in which communists would work with other forces in "civil society", engaging with the parliamentary system (so despised by Lenin) to challenge the ideological "hegemony" of the capitalist governing class.

By the 1970s Italian communists, reacting to the Soviet suppression of efforts to liberalise the Czech Communist Party under Alexander Dubcek as well as to social changes that accompanied the decline of traditional heavy industry, announced a new doctrine of democratic "Eurocommunism". Enjoying the support of one-third of the electorate, the Italian Communist Party began to democratise its own internal life.

In Britain, compared to its continental counterparts, the Communist Party never achieved a similar degree of influence over trade unions — in Britain, after all, the deepest intellectual roots of working-class organisation were in non-conformist protestantism rather than revolutionary socialism. So communists repeatedly (and unsuccessfully) sought influence via electoral alliances with the Labour Party. After Labour prohibited membership of both parties — affecting several councillors and MPs — communists tried to influence Labour through "entryism", that is, discreet infiltration.

From 1945, electoral victory for Labour and its own success in winning two parliamentary seats prompted the Communist Party of Great Britain to elaborate its own "parliamentary road" to socialism. This envisaged the party slowly building elected representation to the point at which it might present itself as an attractive coalition partner for Labour in the event of a hung Parliament. But after 1950 it never regained parliamentary representation and by the 1970s its membership had declined to 18 000.

Where they were most successful, in Italy and France, parliamentary communists looked less and less like revolutionaries. This was hardly surprising in a context that afforded both prosperity and social mobility to the social group they sought to represent, the industrial working class. In general, working classes at best played bit parts in the great 20th-century revolutions; contrary to Marx's predictions, agrarian oppression and the decay of pre-industrial bureaucracies provided much more encouraging environments for radical social revolutions than the citadels of advanced capitalism.

In certain respects, South African communists find themselves in a situation comparable to that of the stronger European parties in the aftermath of World War II. Through their alliance with a dominant national liberation movement and their own contribution to its leadership, ostensibly at least, they may seem to command popularity and influence. Sixty-five communists sit in Parliament as African National Congress members, six belong to President Thabo Mbeki's Cabinet and many more hold electoral office in provincial and local government. In Gauteng, for example, seven out of 10 MECs are believed to be party members. If the South African Communist Party contested elections by itself it would probably win considerably fewer seats than its members hold at present but it might all the same represent a significant force (especially if it enjoyed trade union backing).

But its real resemblance to the more liberal post-war Eurocommunist parties may be in its diminishing commitment to old-fashioned revolutionary socialism — or indeed socialism of any kind — notwithstanding the SACP's base in a traditional industrial working class. To an extent this is the consequence of involvement in a non-socialist government.

Communists can and do defend participation in government by pointing to its reformist achievements — the expansion of welfare entitlements, for example, or the improvement of employment conditions, or even, less convincingly, the pursuit of a "left agenda" by Minister of Public Enterprises Jeff Radebe. In such fields, the contribution of communist legislators and ministers has sometimes been decisive.

As often as not, though, communist Cabinet members as well as parliamentarians find themselves at odds with their party as well as with the trade unions. And can communist MPs really feel comfortable defending arms procurements that divert resources from poverty alleviation or protecting the beneficiaries of bribery by munitions contractors? Do communists sincerely believe today that the government's housing programme — or the crony capitalism represented by black empowerment — signifies a "transformation of power relations in the market" (a phrase used by an optimistic Jeremy Cronin, SACP assistant general secretary, in 1994)? How persuasively can a party undertake its mission "to speak out on behalf of the working class and the poor in particular" while at the same time embracing what it terms a "patriotic bourgeoisie" (whose members it includes in its own leadership)?

Party justifications for its presence in government are understandably defensive. "Comrades in management positions" have as their main "immediate revolutionary" duty to make sure that public funds are "effectively managed". They should also help to isolate and restrain any "counter-revolutionary forces still in our midst". In other words, the socialist project is a holding operation: communists are in power to ensure good government and to keep out reactionaries. It's probably more than communists anywhere else in the world can claim.

That's really the main difference between the present situation of South African communists and any historical antecedents. In the brave new world of post-war Europe, communists could base their hopes on an expanding socialist state system as well as genuine social progress within it. Today local parliamentary socialists can draw cold comfort from geriatric Bolshevik dynasties in Cuba and Korea and a Chinese political autocracy that sanctions truly gross kinds of capitalist exploitation. Without an historically informed sense of destiny, communism loses its point.

July 20 2001

The South African Communist Party celebrated its 80th anniversary in July 2001

NOTES & QUERIES

If Rome wasn't built in a day, how long did it take?

● In 1976 I met an elderly, unrepentant Wobbly — a member of the anarcho-syndicalist Industrial Workers of the World. When I asked him what sustained his political optimism, he replied, "Just remember, young man, Rome wasn't burnt in a day." — *Mark Leier, Canada*

Historians!

Krisjan Lemmer

Lemmer's heart warmed towards the German car-maker BMW when he saw it had volunteered to help sponsor President Thabo Mbeki's project to rewrite South Africa's history. Surfing to BMW's website he noted with approval the multinational's ringing declaration that "BMW does not just stand by its history, but deliberately preserves it as a vital part of its identity."

BMW's account of its rocket-manufacturing activities under the Third Reich is notably brief. Strangely, no reference is to be found on the site to the more recent contribution made by the company to the German fund for the compensation of slave and forced labourers. Surely such generosity should not be allowed to pass unnoticed?

March 30 2001

Colour me yellow

Thuli Nhlapo

I am known as Thuli. In full my name is Thulisile Ennie. *Thulisile* means a state of quietness. Grandmother — the mother of the man who is married to my mother, and the same man I grew up thinking was my father — gave me the name when I joined her family.

I was spared the details but my mother was pregnant before she married my father. No one wanted to disclose when exactly lobola was paid for my mother. What my mother told me was that she hated being pregnant with me before she was married because it was "not a good thing" for her and her family.

Granny didn't like the name my mother's parents gave me when I was born — Khabonina. *Khabo* means home and *nina* means mother. It was an appropriate name because I was born at my mother's home, but it was changed.

Granny named me Thulisile, after revisiting events surrounding my birth. She was told I had been quiet the whole day and then suddenly my mother went into labour during the early hours of May 11 1970. Perhaps in pretending that I was a full member of her family at Tsebe — a place situated between Hebron and Klipgat near Pretoria — granny pronounced me Ennie. That was her name.

I must have been five years old when I realised that no one called me Thuli or Thulisile. My nickname was, and still is, Tho. Granny called me Mabovana — referring to my light complexion. There was nothing wrong with that. My mother and I were the only light-skinned members of the family. The others were either a little bit dark or pitch black. Even though I didn't mind, because I did not understand, I noticed that three of my aunts and the older children referred to me as *boesman.*

It was in 1977, when I started schooling at Tlo-Tlo Mpho Primary School in Ga-Rankuwa, that I became convinced that something was terribly wrong with me. My teacher, Mam Ncanywa, never called anyone by their name, but if I dared not wipe my slate properly she would refer to me as "this yellow thing" or "you're so yellow like a pumpkin". I learned to get everything right the first time to avoid being called yellow. Four of my cousins attended Tlo-Tlo Mpho Primary School. We used the same school bus. Our homes were in the same yard. Mother's husband paid all our school fees, but as soon as home was no longer in sight we were strangers. I followed behind, remembering not to share a seat in the bus with any of them. The *boesman* issue was getting worse, even though I still didn't know the meaning of the word.

I began to get closer to its meaning during an incident one Thursday. I remember because that was "Sheila's day". My three aunts were domestic workers while my mother was a housewife, so they brought sweets back from work. By that time my younger sister was three years old and the darling of the family. The family kraal name, Sgegede Samathole, was reserved for her only, but, again, I did not see anything wrong with that.

When all the kids ran to the second aunt who was coming home from work, I followed them. She gave them, including the neighbours' children, sweets. My younger sister, who stood before me, got her share. When it was my turn, with my shy smile and brown eyes, I looked down with both hands in a receiving gesture. Instead of the aunt pouring sweets into my hands, she shouted, "Nx! Go away, you *boesman.* I don't have sweets for white things. Go and tell your drunk *boesman* aunts to buy you sweets. By the way, where is your white mother?"

I had been called that word before but it had never hurt as much as it did the day I was turned away from sweets and told in front of the other kids that something was wrong with me.

I was used to playing alone, drawing people on the ground. Those were my friends. I told them what to say and I made them like me. One day that same year my cousin Gqibo called me. I was in my favourite spot next to the main gate and my cousins were playing next to the garage with the other kids. I was puzzled when Gqibo said: "Ja, let's fight," because I was not a fighter and she was older than me. My big cousin, Phumu, loaded sand in both her hands and closed them in fists. The practice was done to determine who was a coward. The first person to pound the fist was considered brave.

The group was cheering. I was hoping the characters I drew on the ground would come to my rescue when Gqibo punched my face. "Aye ye ye *boesman*!" "Look she's turned blue!" "No, look she's turning red!" It was obvious that the crowd was excited to see a fight between a normal person and a *boesman*. The punches rained on my mouth, stomach and face. I was about to fall down but Gqibo picked me up and shoved me under her left arm where she punched my face to her satisfaction.

I never cried but when she let go of me I fell to the ground and felt the earth rotate. The group was still cheering. I felt an urgent need to wipe my nose but there was blood on my hand. "Oh look," shouted one girl in the group, "she's got red blood. I thought *boesmen* have a different colour. It's not red like ours. See, it's weak. This thing has green veins — so what makes you think it can have the same blood like ours?"

I could not afford to mess my clothes. My mother was going to be hysterical. Worse still, how was I to explain what happened? She was not going to believe me. Even if she did she was going to tell her husband, who would say I was lying, and shout and swear at me. That was what happened when I told my mother that my cousin Phumu had pierced my bicycle tyres with a nail. My mother believed me but my father was angry.

I was down and defeated but the crowd did not disperse. Perhaps they wanted to observe how *boesmen* stood up after being beaten. Stand up I did, but I had to balance myself on the nearest wall before standing up to my cousin Gqibo. "One day I'm going to be old. I'm going to be strong and rich. You'll come to me for help but I'm going to turn you away." "You won't be rich with my uncle's money that you and your mother are wasting. And listen, *boesman*, I will never ask anything from you because there will be nothing to ask for," said Gqibo.

Since all my attempts to be accepted were unsuccessful, I gave up. It was useless to try to smile when I knew I was not wanted. That was when I forgot what it was like to smile. A frown and a serious look became a mask that I wear to this day. My favourite spot next to the main gate was abandoned. I was afraid my cousins might kill me without anyone knowing.

Silently, I started reading every book I came across, from my seTswana books to the South Sotho Bible and cousin Tom's Zulu books. I could neither cry nor play; I had to keep my mind busy. I started helping my mother wash the dishes after serving the family meals. Granny was not unaware of how I was treated. She had her own way of ill-treating me. It was tradition that every day at one o'clock she would be served tea and brown bread with butter on the veranda. All the kids would join in. If I ate all the food, "Mabovana was eating like a pig"; but if I did not want to participate, Mabovana would be "too full of herself because she thinks she's better than us".

But one thing was certain: Mabovana or *boesman*, I got first class in sub-standard A and B. Some of my cousins came in last and some had to repeat their grades.

I never knew we were leaving Pretoria until a big red lorry stood outside the gate. Our furniture was loaded and I, my mother, younger sister, younger brother and my mother's husband followed behind in a car. We must have travelled for days before we stopped in the middle of a forest. That was Fernie, a village in Mpumalanga, more than 90km from Ermelo.

People spoke siSwati in this region and we had to learn to communicate with them. Mother and I used too many Afrikaans words. She is Ndebele and that is how her people talk. I switched from seTswana to siSwati and continued to hold the first place in class at Dinga Primary School. I had always been convinced that my mother's husband was my real father. I even found similar features in the two of us. I had blamed his indifference and bad temper on granny and his sisters. But now that we were away from his family and he was nasty to me, I started questioning my origins.

I wanted to earn my own money instead of depending on him. For my first small business I bought a pack of peanuts and fried them in water after sprinkling them with salt. The business operated from a yellow and white container that I carried with me to school. A teaspoon was 3c. In an attempt to make more money, I sold oranges in winter and continued to sell the peanuts, with my schoolwork improving with each term. Mother bought us savings boxes and mine served as my bank. Before falling asleep every night, I would fantasise about who my real father might be. For reasons I could not explain I was convinced he was rich and understood me.

On the few occasions that I had a conversation with my mother's husband, he was either reprimanding me or threatening to beat me up with his belt. He was never satisfied with my schoolwork. If I was first in class, he would complain about my low aggregate marks. If I came second, he would ask where I was when the top pupil was being taught. To my younger sister, who was not that gifted, father would sing praises of how hard she had worked after coming 20th in class.

I helped this man to pull up fences. I was his assistant mechanic — I used to hand him tools as he worked — and I made sure his car was washed before he returned to Germiston, where he drove long-distance trucks. Then I found out that he was cheating on my mother. I read a letter his girlfriend wrote. He kept it in the sideboard drawer. My mother had dusted there and shifted the letter many times but she could not read and write so she never knew what was inside the envelope. I hated all men. I concluded they were all mean cheaters. I doubled my efforts at having my own money.

I learned how to knit table mats, Babygros, hats and scarves and to fashion doormats with grass. I sold some of those items and saved the money. Father started staying away from home for months and I had to help my mother keep the family going. She sold vegetables and made dresses. I would balance a big dish of cabbages on my head after school and on weekends and go from door to door selling them. While some people would buy, others would send me away and dogs barked at me, but I continued to sell.

Fernie is a beautiful place with rocks shaped in different ways, mountains, forests and the Methula river. After a day of hard work, I would take a walk down to the river because I loved the sound of water hitting the rocks. Looking into the water calmed my troubled nerves. Even though no one called me names at Fernie, I was looking for every little piece of information about *boesmen* — and about the man I was convinced was my real father.

I had read numerous Zulu books such as *Umbuso kaShaka, uNada noMhlophekazi to Izwi nesithunzi* and *Imiyalezo*. Nothing was mentioned about *boesmen* in these books. In all prescribed Siswati books I read at school, no author said a thing about boesmen. All I had picked up at that stage was that *boesmen* were kids born of black mothers who had been raped by white men.

Granny eventually left Pretoria to live at Fernie with some cousins. There must have been nine in all. Her house was not in our yard but across the Methula river. Perhaps it was poverty that made granny soften up on me — or was it my fame? From across the river to the households near the pine trees, the name Ennie Nhlapo, the light-skinned girl, rang a bell for many people. Because many people in this community were from farms, most children were too old for the grades they were in. I was leading the way as the cleverest girl in the village.

I crossed the river to stay with granny and learned many lessons about life. When the toothpaste was finished and funds were low, we used salt to brush our teeth. When there was no money for bread, we ate pap and black tea for breakfast, lunch and supper. We would cook pap and add the fat we had saved from cooking if we did not have money for meat or vegetables.

Girl cousins who were menstruating, and I joined them when my time came, used the old newspapers that came from the white madams' houses where their mothers worked in Pretoria. Every evening granny would tell us stories around the small stove. She taught us how to talk to God — many people call it praying.

I made it to Simtfolile High School. The number of cousins staying with granny was reduced when some fell pregnant and had to go back to their mothers in Pretoria. I was 16 years old and in standard eight, still a top pupil in science classes, and things were going well when granny took ill. Before she was taken to the hospital she told me things she thought were important, such as staying away from boys, studying more and looking after the three remaining cousins when she was gone.

I took advantage of the situation and asked her one more time: "What is my real surname and who is my father?" She never answered, but for the first time she didn't get angry at my question. She looked at me for a very long time before saying I must go to sleep and take care of myself after she was gone.

Granny passed away, leaving me with R23 to take care of my three young cousins. To cope, I wrote myself a poem. I added the baking of scones to the business I was running just to make ends meet. We moved to my mother's home but things got worse financially. My last-born sister was five years old and mother was spending most of her time in her room. For the first time I did not do well at school.

In 1988 I left Fernie for Soshanguve in Pretoria to give myself a better chance at passing my matric. It was at Reitumetse High School that Professor CT Msimang — then head of Unisa's African languages department and now acting registrar — came to visit the standard 10 Zulu class. I was excellent in writing essays and analysing literature. The only challenge was that siSwati was different from isiZulu. I had to put more effort into mastering the language. The professor was shown some of my work and he advised me to do a BA, majoring in Zulu, because he thought I would do well as a Zulu writer. I didn't take him seriously, which was why I went to Technikon Northern Gauteng after matriculating.

Mother's husband paid my fees for the first year and I had a bursary after that. I was never given money for toiletries, so granny's way of living came in handy when toothpaste and New Freedom pads were not available, and I collected pieces of soap in the bathrooms left by wealthy students.

I stayed with my mother's sister and her husband in Soshanguve, but was told to leave after my uncle saw my tracksuit on the washing line. Since it was a family of born-again Christians, I was not supposed to wear pants. I was training in karate and couldn't do it in a skirt, but my uncle didn't understand, so I left and found a room on campus.

The second semester I stayed with my mother's brother, who asked me to leave at the end of the year. He had encouraged me to have a boyfriend — he even insisted that I visit him at his home. It was fine with him as long as he knew where I was. But he expelled me the morning I came home. In 1991 I stayed with my father's brother and his wife. I had learned not to trust anyone so I kept a room on campus and came "home" on weekends.

It was in 1991 that mother's husband complained that I was not visiting Fernie anymore. His sister-in-law said that as I was about to complete my studies my father wanted me to return home to get a job and give him money. Without discussing my intentions with anyone I decided that I had to leave Soshanguve for a place where I had no relatives, and I moved to Durban.

In 1992 at Mangosuthu Technikon I met a handsome boy and got pregnant, irrespective of the fact that I had never missed a single contraceptive pill. I wrote the event in my diary and my aunt read it when I went back to Soshanguve during Easter holidays. A family meeting was called with my mother and her husband present. Mother did not protect me when her husband disowned me and said he never wanted to see me in his home again. His brother tried to talk some sense into his head but he was told to shut up. His sister-in-law, who had been convinced that at 22 I was not going to have kids, did not want me in her house either. I was the first in the family to matriculate and the first girl to turn 18 without having had a child, but those facts were not considered.

I left for Mangosuthu with my bulging stomach and the R200 I had earned at South African Breweries for temporary work. Six kilometres from Durban the minibus taxi rolled. The day I spent at Greys hospital in Pietermaritzburg delayed me so all the rooms in residence were occupied when I got to the technikon. I had to squat in a room with 12 other students for the semester.

During the Gqozo massacre the technikon was closed and the students went home. I had nowhere to go and no money so I stayed on campus and drank water for seven days. My boyfriend not only dumped me but paraded his other girlfriends on campus. I was determined to write exams irrespective of all those challenges. To keep myself from going insane I wrote a poem that I recited to my baby every time I felt like crying or giving up.

When I completed writing exams I was wondering where I was supposed to go when an elderly woman from KwaNdebele said she would take me to her house. But I never got there. At the end of the weekend I packed my bags and went to the hospital to get my file from my doctor — I had used my bursary money to buy maternity dresses and to attend antenatal classes. The doctor checked me and sent me straight to the labour ward because the baby was on his way. It took three nights, two full days and two stitches and then my baby, a boy, was born.

I arranged for my luggage to be taken to the baby's father's home. His good mother came to see me in the hospital and said she would talk to my parents while keeping myself and the baby at her house. But my parents would not listen to her argument that we were kids who had made a mistake and had to be forgiven.

The father of my child continually verbally abused me, with girlfriends coming in and out of the house. He must have recruited quite a few for the purpose because there were many.

After three weeks I left Durban for a shack near Zonkizizwe in Germiston that was our home for five months. With help from friends I managed to cook porridge that I ate through the day while breastfeeding my baby. He was five months old when I got a job as an administrative assistant at the Singapore embassy in Johannesburg. When we graduated from the shack to a flat in Berea, my mother came looking for us. She was not sorry, but I was employed and it made sense for her to want to look after my baby. I opted for a domestic worker instead.

I wrote a collection of 10 poems in 1994 sitting on my bed in the flat after putting my baby to sleep. Two of them, one about granny's funeral and another about my son, were chosen for a Zulu anthology and published in 1995.

It became more and more obvious that my father was not my real father. I tried to visit at month ends but found it difficult to tolerate him. He demanded money from me because he had brought me up. I refused because by then I was saving for a townhouse in Fourways. He called me a bitch who did not want to get married because I wanted to sleep with other women's husbands in my house.

I bought a brand-new car and he failed to congratulate me. My novels, written at night in siSwati, were winning prizes — *Sibono Sabo* won second prize in 1995 in the African Heritage Awards, which *Imbali Yemangcamane* won the following year — but my family did not care because I had refused to pay them for having brought me up. Yet when his favourite girl — my younger sister — got pregnant at 18 he took leave to be there for her, sent her back to school and blamed me for being a bad example.

His last-born daughter fell pregnant at age 17 in 1999 and he never opened his mouth. I pay her bills — baby clothes, baby formula, the wage of a domestic worker to look after him while her mother attends school in Ermelo.

My son wanted a brother and I wanted another baby — but not a marriage — so I had another baby boy in April 1998. I was happy and am still excited about my two handsome boys who are from different fathers. We are going to have another brother or sister because we are going to be a normal family, whether I am married or not.

My having a second baby was the final straw in my fragile relationship with my mother's husband. The day I went home with the baby, who had been born prematurely at six months, he insulted me in a manner I decided was not to be tolerated. He was not financially responsible for me, so why all the fuss? We have not met since that incident.

My little one must have been two months old when I left on a fact-finding mission. I had to find my real father and, after years of pestering, I was given the address of a house in Standerton. Because the house is in the suburbs, it was easy to pretend to be looking for something along that street.

Funny, the people who came out of the house were a white man, his wife and two boys, who must have been about 17 and 20. It made no sense to me, so I phoned the person who had given me the address. He was furious. He said if I had questions, I must ask the man I had seen at the house. I realised I preferred not to know. I went back to Johannesburg but it was no use. My milk had dried up, I'd lost my appetite, I could not sleep, I suffered from headaches. The doctor said it was post-natal depression.

I was still on maternity leave, so I went back to Standerton. This time I waited for the man to drive in and I knocked at the door. One of the boys opened the door and I asked to speak to an adult. A white man came to the door. I was hurting so deeply and was so anxious to meet this man that when he approached my eyes were glued to him. Perhaps he said hello but I did not hear the words because I was looking straight into his eyes. His eyes studied me carefully. I did not say a word. We stood there looking at each other until the boy who opened the door came back, maybe to check why his daddy was clutching the door and looking at the black girl standing in the doorway. His daddy sent him away.

After what seemed like ages the white man came out of the door and directed me to sit down on the garden chairs. We sat and, after taking a deep breath, he said: "Your mother is ...?" It was my mother's name. I had braced myself for the worst but I could not hold back the tears from streaming down my cheeks. He was sweating but went on to say, more to himself than to me: *"Here, my kind* [God, my child]."

I wailed. He was about to touch my hand when I jumped up and went straight to the gate. He must have been saying I should wait but I couldn't take it. I closed the gate behind me but I was dizzy and felt the need to sit down on the lawn. I vomited. The car came out the yard and stopped near where I was sitting. I was too weak to run away so the man picked me up and put me on the back seat. He drove so fast I thought he was going to kill me but I did not care. That was better than having a white Afrikaner father. I thought my wish was coming true when he stopped at a secluded area and quickly came to sit next to me on the back seat. I even thought this white man was going to rape me but he was holding me for dear life and sobbing like a baby.

After he calmed down, he told me he was my father. He said he had known about the pregnancy but had been scared of his father. He said the laws of the country did not allow him to love across the colour line. He said he knew what I was thinking but it was far from that because he said he had loved my mother.

He asked if I was 29 years old and I nodded my head. He said he had never forgotten about me; he had always counted how old I was supposed to be. He begged for my forgiveness, and that was when I asked him to take me to the taxi rank.

I hated my white father because I suspected he had raped my mother. I had heard stories of white men experimenting with black women. I had narrowly escaped rape twice by white men — one in Pretoria and one in Sandton. I regretted leaving my gun in Johannesburg because I wanted to kill him.

He did not argue with me and drove to the taxi rank. He scribbled telephone numbers on a piece of paper and I was even more disgusted to discover that my surname started with an O. It was a typical Afrikaans surname and I hated it.

I went back to my boys and tried to live a normal life but I lost weight rapidly and eventually went to my GP. She understood me, perhaps because she had been my doctor since 1994. She called a psychiatrist and booked an appointment for that afternoon. She said I was depressed.

It was after two weeks at a psychiatric ward, two weeks of leaving my boys with their Indian nanny, two weeks of lying to the occupational therapist, the psychologist and the psychiatrist that my problems were my job and being disowned by my parents, that I decided I was going to accept that my father was a white Afrikaner. The occupational therapist suggested I leave my job and tell her what it was that I loved to do. I told her I wanted to write another book — but a non-fiction one about my life.

After I was discharged from hospital I started freelancing as a journalist for *True Love* and *Sunday World*, and there were interviews about my books on Radio Metro and Yfm. I even appeared on *Thari* on SABC, discussing the challenges of being a young black published and award-winning author.

I was awarded a Steve Biko scholarship and went to Grahamstown to work for no pay at the *East Cape News*. It must have been the environment in the Eastern Cape but I made up my mind to call my father. His wife answered and demanded to know who I was and why I wanted to speak to her husband. I said something about a policy and she called him. I said two words, "It's fine," and he understood what I really meant. He gave his cellphone number and suggested I call him.

Back in Johannesburg I decided to confront my mother. I was not rude to her but asked her who my real father was. She cried for the whole weekend, saying I was crazy and the man she married was my father. She said I was ungrateful after he had brought me up. I gave up on getting any explanation from her.

That was just more than two years ago. My real father and I have spent some time together — he even taught me how to fish during one of our weekends away — and I love him and I know he loves me. I have met my white stepmother and my eldest half-brother, who is practising as a lawyer. It will take time to prepare my own boys to meet their white grandfather and uncles.

My real father insisted on buying me a car and a bigger house and giving me some money but I refused all of it. He did not understand that I was not doing it to punish him but simply that I am used to working hard for everything I have, no matter how small and insignificant. Because he is running his own company, he is very proud of his only girl's little achievements.

We are still fighting because he wants me to reconcile with my mother's husband, whom I last saw two years ago. Whenever I go to visit my mother I make sure he is not around. I do not get told family news but I get phoned if money is needed. My real father says he wants to meet my mother's husband but I do not think it would be a good idea.

It was sad at first but it is true that my surname starts with an O. I am not 100% black and not 100% white. My father and half-brothers might have straight hair and blue eyes but we are all human beings with a heart and a soul and that is what matters, at least to me.

The day the people of South Africa learn to judge one another on character rather than the colour of their skin, I would say we are free at last because no child will be punished – for being a *boesman*.

November 20 2000

A close encounter with Mr Why

John Matshikiza

The Blue Moon Café in downtown Dakar is a funky sort of place, the interior designed to resemble the inside of a passenger aircraft, with the clientele, on a busy night, crushed together in the economy-class seats, staring out of the windows of an aircraft that is going nowhere, drinking cocktails and listening to the beat. You can meet anybody there.

The other night it happened to be a white boy from Indiana, who had his hair styled like the last of the Mohicans, only in blond. Jude had an interesting take on the world in general, which boiled down to a sense of contempt for all boundaries and nationalities, and a laid-back certainty about his own right to freedom of movement. For the past 12 years he had been moving round Africa.

Jude's African adventures had begun with a stint in the Peace Corps in Kenya. From there he had just kept floating round the continent, hitching on to situations as and when he pleased: standing on the sidelines during South Africa's low-intensity war against anti-apartheid forces in Lesotho in the 1980s; getting married and unmarried in Zambia; one thing here, another thing there, until he had finally fetched up here in Dakar, running a computer hardware and software outlet and just, you know, like, hanging out.

He was a funny looking juba. Apart from that yellow tuft at the front of his head ("Who does your hair?" I asked. "I do it myself, in the bathroom," he replied looking at me with a, like, "Wow, that was a real dumb question" kind of look) he had an unusually long, sharp nose and a narrow chin, and was sporting an unflattering pair of spectacles that would have appeared, at first glance, to do nothing to improve his prospects. Nevertheless, he walked into the Blue Moon with a stunning black babe in tow. Or rather, she walked in with him in tow.

As fate would have it, we knew the black babe. She was a bit taken aback to find us there, but she gladly accepted our invitation to join our table, and dragged Jude along with her. Which is how we came to find ourselves in conversation (if you can call it that) with Jude.

We soon found out that Jude didn't give a shit about anything. The first thing he didn't give a shit about was what country he was in, or the language that people spoke there. He thought languages were a waste of time. On the other hand, he never allowed himself to be pinned down on the question of whether English, which is what we were all, sort of, like, speaking, was a language in the same sense, or not.

The waiter came and took our orders, in French. Jude ordered vodka with a slice of lemon, in English. He and the waiter stared at each other in mutual incomprehension until we stepped in and translated. "Whew, what's his problem?" said Jude as the waiter walked away. "You've been here two years," said the stunning black babe. "How come you still don't speak any French? Not even enough to be able to ask for a slice of lemon?"

"Why?" Jude retorted. "I didn't come here to talk French, I came here to do computers. Besides," he continued, "is French a Senegalese language? Why should I talk to anyone in French in Senegal? Senegal is in Africa, not in France." He smiled at us condescendingly, having dismissed a couple of hundred years of colonial baggage that still had us foxed in half a minute.

"So how about Senegalese languages," the babe shot back. "Would you know how to order a slice of lemon in Wolof? Or maybe Toucouleur?" "Why?" asked Jude, shaking his head in amazement. "Why should I get hung up about languages?"

I've heard about Dr No, but I'd never come across Mr Why before. Everything that we regarded as logical, he regarded as outrageous, puerile or threatening. His standard answer was "Why?" Which made you wonder why he was constantly backing himself so far up a lonely cul-de-sac. "Why? Why? Why?"

"So why Africa?" we asked. "Why?" he replied. "I can be anywhere I want." "So why not America?" "Why?" "OK, why not Mongolia, then?" "Mongolia? Why?"

It was useless to try and play the conversation game with this guy, just like it's useless to try and play a game of poker with someone who insists on being dealt in but then refuses to call, pass or stack. Just sits there with a hand of cards and laughs at everybody else for indulging in a game with dumb rules.

We got to him, though, when he decided that it was time for him and the babe to go and see someone off at the airport, at this late hour of the night. "You go," I said to him. "The babe stays." The babe, amazingly, agreed. "You'll find me here when you get back," she said. "Why do I need to go all the way to the airport to see off someone I don't know?"

Jude stared at her, then at us, disconcerted for the first time that evening. Maybe for the first time in his life. "I'll be about an hour," he said as he rose to his feet. "Don't do anything silly," he warned as he fled for the door.

He was back in less than an hour. He was amazed to find his babe untouched. He sat for a few more nervous minutes, and then took her out of there, keeping the babe on a very tight leash indeed.

So it turned out that there are some rules that Jude is prepared to fight for. Rules of engagement with babes is one. But I guess you'd have to dig real deep to find out what the rest are. It might not even be worth it.

November 3 2000

NOTES & QUERIES

Do we need critics?

● Of course we need critics. How else could we employ thousands of failed writers, artists, musicians, et cetera? — *David Lewis, Ferney-Voltaire, France*

● The answer can be derived from the language of the question. Why "we", a term that implies solidarity between questioner and replier in a common attitude towards critics? Why not a detached "Does one need critics?" or an abstract "Are critics necessary?" Similarly, why "need"? Is necessity the test that critics must meet to justify their existence? Might it not be enough that we liked them, were interested by them — even amused? The question is a verbal three-card trick. It identifies the constituency to which it is addressed, namely those whose opinions are conditioned by a desire that they be part of the majority ("we"). It supplies the answer ("We don't need critics") by setting the extreme test of necessity as the criterion of a correct response. It is a question only in the form of its language. In its subtext it is a confession of the author's doubts about his ability to judge cultural artefacts, and his suspicions about pundits; and it is an appeal to like-minded persons to confirm his opinion by showing it is shared by the majority. Still, the question is expressed pithily and wittily, and the subject is of continuing interest to everyone. I couldn't stop laughing. This question will run and run. A topic for all the family. — *Jim Williams, Stockport*

The dignity of the black body

Njabulo S Ndebele

I confess to being one of those who have had an ambivalent attitude towards the recent national conference on racism. On the one hand, I welcomed the attention paid to this national problem of racism. On the other hand, I remain deeply worried about the terms on which the problem was highlighted and engaged.

I am bothered by the phenomenon of a black majority in power seeming to reduce itself to the status of complainants, as if they had a limited capacity to do anything more significant about the situation at hand than drawing attention to it. It is not that the complaints have no foundation; on the contrary, the foundations are deeply embedded in our history. But I cannot shake off the feeling that the galvanising of concern around racism reflects a vulnerability that could dangerously resuscitate a familiar psychology of inferiority, precisely at the moment that the black majority ought to provide confident leadership through the government they have elected.

I worry that the complaining may confusingly look like a psychological submission to "whiteness" in the sense of handing over to "whiteness" the power to provide relief. "Please, stop this thing!" seems to be the appeal. "Respect us." I submit that we moved away from this position decisively on April 27 1994. We cannot go back to it. It should not be so easy to give up a psychological advantage.

I am bothered by the tendency that when a black body is dragged down the road behind a bakkie, we see first proof of racism rather than depravity and murder; as if, if the causal link between racism and murder could not be established, the gruesome killing might not attract as much attention. When we give to racism in Africa this kind of centrality of explanation, we confirm the status of the black body as a mere item of data to be deployed in a grammar of political argument, rather than affirm it as violated humanity.

The inherent worth of a black body does not need to be affirmed by the mere proof of white racism against it. The black body is much more than the cruelty to which it is subjected. If we succeed in positioning ourselves as a people, above this kind of cruelty, we deny it equality of status. We can then deal with it as one among many other problems in our society that need our attention.

I think this is what Steve Biko meant when he cautioned against "the major danger" he saw "facing the black community — be so conditioned by the system as to make even our most well-considered resistance to it fit within the system both in terms of the means and of the goals". It is possible we are not entirely out of this danger.

Is the foregrounding of race and racism a veiled admission that perhaps there is as yet no material basis for the black majority to contain this scourge through the imposition of it own versions of the future? Does this speak to the black majority's perception that perhaps they are not yet agents of history? I ask these questions in the knowledge that white racism in South Africa no longer exists as a formalised structure. We conjure in our minds the continued existence of such a structure to our perceptual peril.

There is no evidence of a Ku Klux Klan that is regrouping somewhere in the far-flung corners of the country. On the contrary, with the disintegration of apartheid as a formal structure, white racism has reacted in a number of ways. In some cases it has simply died. In other cases, particularly where strong pockets of white power remain, such as in commerce, industry and in higher education, it has either mutated and assumed the colour of change while retaining a core of self-interest, or has genuinely struggled with the agonies of embracing necessary change. In other cases, racism also continues to exist as individualised pathology, frequently exploding into acts of suicide or desperate acts of brutality against black bodies in sight. In almost every case, we witness a crisis of identity with various degrees of intensity.

But what these various forms of reaction do show is the danger inherent in a singular approach. That is why the black majority carries the historic responsibility to provide, in this situation, decisive and visionary leadership. Either it embraces this responsibility with conviction, or it gives up its leadership through a throwback psychological dependence on racism which has the potential to severely compromise the authority conferred on it by history. What is the connection between the critique of "whiteness" and what our response to it has been; the hegemonic growth of a black consciousness (not in the sense of a philosophy or movement associated with Steve Biko, although it may not exclude it, but rather, in the more fundamental sense of the inevitability of a particular kind of social process); and the project of development so essential to our finding the future?

It will be obvious that the flow of social influence is not going in one direction from the black to the white community. There is a two-way process setting itself up as a critical stabilising factor, as we negotiate change.

Because the process will not always be smooth, it will require a great deal of negotiated positions.

On balance, though, white South Africa will be called upon to make greater adjustments to black needs than the other way round. This is an essential condition for a shift in white identity in which "whiteness" can undergo an experiential transformation by absorbing new cultural experience as an essential condition for achieving a new sense of cultural rootedness. That is why every white South African should be proud to speak, read and write at least one African language, and be ashamed if they are not able to.

This matter of rootedness is important. For example, from a black perspective, whatever the economic merits of the case, it is difficult not to see the transfer of capital to big Western stock exchanges as "whiteness" delinking itself from the mire of its South African history, to explore opportunities of disengagement, where the home base is transformed into a satellite market revolving around powerful Western economies, to become a market to be exploited rather than a home to be served. This kind of "flight of white capital" may represent white abandonment of responsibility towards the only history that can promise salvation to "whiteness".

"Whiteness" has a responsibility to demonstrate its bona fides in this regard. Where is the primary locus of responsibility for white capital, built over centuries with black labour and unjust laws? A failure to come to terms with the morality of this question ensures the continuation of the culture of insensitivity and debilitating guilt. In the past "whiteness" proclaimed its civilising mission in Africa. In reality, any advantages for black people, where they occurred, were an unintended result rather than an intended objective.

A historic opportunity has arisen now for white South Africa to participate in a humanistic revival of our country through a readiness to participate in the process of redress and reconciliation. This is on the understanding that the "heart of whiteness" will be hard put to reclaim its humanity without the restoration of dignity to the black body.

We are all familiar with the global sanctity of the white body. Wherever the white body is violated in the world, severe retribution follows somehow for the perpetrators, if they are non-white, regardless of the social status of the white body. The white body is inviolable, and that inviolability is in direct proportion to the global vulnerability of the black body.

This leads me to think that if South African whiteness is a beneficiary of the protectiveness assured by international whiteness, it has an opportunity to write a new chapter in world history. It will have to come out from under the umbrella and repudiate it. Putting itself at risk, it will have to declare that it is home now, sharing in the vulnerability of other compatriot bodies. South African whiteness will declare that its dignity is inseparable from the dignity of black bodies.

The collapse of "white leadership" that would spearhead this process has been lamented. On second thoughts, perhaps this situation represents a singular opportunity. The collapse of "white leadership" ought to lead to the collapse of the notion of "black leadership". Where there is no "white leadership" to contest with "black leadership", where these descriptions of leadership were a function of an outmoded politics of a racist state, we are left only with leaders to lead this country. There can be no more compelling argument than this, to urge for care and caution in addressing the issue of racism in the southern tip of the African continent.

The historic disintegration of "white leadership" imposes immense responsibilities on how we frame notions of leadership in the resultant political space we are now inheriting. This way, the South African state is placed in a unique position to declare its obligations to all citizens. It should jealously and vigorously protect all bodies within its borders and beyond.

September 15 2000

NOTES & QUERIES

Why are teenagers bored?

● So that rings can be inserted into the holes. — *Andrew Wardrop, London*

● The "teenager" is a new phenomenon. In Neanderthal times teenagers were the hunter/gatherers. Nature programmed us so that we reached our mental, physical and sexual peaks during the teenage years, with most people dying before 40. As life became easier childhood became longer and we had time and energy to spare. Society has developed so that teenagers now have all the instincts to go out into the world and "fight" for a living, but few opportunities to do so. They have three choices: to find studies or hobbies that absorb their "survival" instincts; to go through a wild "raging hormone" stage; or to attempt to kill off the instinct with drink, drugs and so on. Boredom is nature's way of saying: "Do something." — *Stan Hayward, London*

● I don't care. — *Sietse Brouwer (14), Bennekom, The Netherlands*

Give 'em the old razzle-dazzle

Robert Kirby

Blessed are the meek and mild for they shall inherit the presidential television interview. Thabo Mbeki must have been well pleased e.tv sent along a pair of such vapid bozos with a set of such predictable questions. San Reddy and Debora Patta were a sort of clown duo doing a routine as "no nonsense" interrogators, their essential smarminess leaking through every crack. A perfect occasion for the disporting of some virtuoso Mbeki-style flim-flam-flooey. As the song from Chicago goes: "Give 'em the old razzle-dazzle, bead and flummox 'em/ How can they see with stardust in their eyes?"

The technique — if technique isn't too spacious a term — behind the Patta/Reddy interviewing was plain to see. By asking what sound like difficult questions the impression is given that the questioners are serious about what they're doing. But they never take anything further. They ask a penetrating question, receive an assiduously fatuous answer and then, as Reddy would say, change focus.

On more than several occasions Mbeki was asked questions in response to which he obfuscated, strayed off the point, blathered on or just plain avoided answering. For nearly all the time Patta and Reddy failed to follow through on their questions. They let Mbeki get away with as much as he wanted to get away with, to include some truly preposterous statements and misdirection. To be fair, Patta did push a bit when asking about the Zimbabwe debacle but avoided asking the obvious question: if Mr Mbeki is so adamant about not interfering in the domestic affairs of neighbouring countries, how does he justify the armed invasion by his government of Lesotho? Keep it up your sleeve for next time, Debora.

After a couple of years of horrendous publicity about the South African presidency it is quite plain to see that Mbeki has decided to play ardent swain to the media, to get into the political spin game with a vengeance. If you can't beat 'em, fondle 'em; in the light of which it is a bit odd Mbeki chose to prattle on like a back-fence gossip about how the South African media need to be more professional. Mind you, with Tony Heard as his closest-to-hand example of a big-time South African hack, I'm not surprised he's a bit dubious about the profession as a whole.

Most diverting was to watch the president fulminating away about the reported anti-Mbeki lobby in his ranks — coincidentally Shades Tshwete had just named some of them on SABC television. These pretenders to his throne should be courageous and honest enough to come out into the open, said Mbeki, his face wreathed in distress at the thought of some mambas in his grass — black ones to boot and therefore cancelling out any possible cries of racism as being the guiding impulse.

It was all very wry coming from someone whose whole style of administration is deeply conspiratorial. I also wondered why neither Reddy nor Patta thought to ask Mbeki to speculate on African coups d'ètat in general. Should this pale attempt at one be seen as the first of many that will bloom under the rainbow?

If anything at all came out of this interview it was that the South African state president is very bad at communicating and very good at relentless sophomoric windiness. He's also more than a little out of touch — he didn't know about the upcoming Job Summit. Everything Mbeki says is cloaked in a sort of waxen conditionality. He's always "looking at the needs" or "seeking possibilities" or his election favourite, "accelerating the process of change", like one of those asinine characters in reformation comedies — Lord Fizzalot?

There were a couple of real treasures. Asked whether he would set an example by undergoing an Aids test, the president's reply was, "No, it would be setting an example within the context of a particular paradigm" — and here we all were thinking it was just a case of letting some admittedly Westernised expert have a close peep at a few drops of your blood. Later the pres came out with, "In the process of accelerating the process of change ..." By any measure the above are state-of-the-art gobbledegook. Not so for Patta and Reddy who drank it all in with little murmurs of approval.

That song from Chicago could finish: "They'll think you're wise and democratic/ Long as your lies are all emphatic/ Razzle-dazzle 'em and they'll never get wise."

May 4 2001

NOTES & QUERIES

Was Viagra the biggest nine-day wonder in history?
● You kept it up for nine days? — *Thomas, Marina da Gama, Cape Town*

A disastrous reign

Editorial (Howard Barrell)

Several years ago we asked the same question: Is Thabo Mbeki fit to rule? At the time, it elicited a furious response from African National Congress representatives and a coterie of others keen to ingratiate themselves with the heir apparent to Nelson Mandela. It was deemed an unfitting question, insulting, arrogant and — predictably — racist.

Today we ask the question again. And we can be certain that, again, it will draw shrill cries from the praise-singers in the presidency. But this time we ask it in the knowledge that it is on the lips of many South Africans, many of them dedicated members of the ANC, the South African Communist Party and the trade unions. Is Mbeki fit to rule?

His 22 months in power have been disastrous. And he has no one to blame but himself. Whether in his dealings with the Aids crisis — surely the gravest threat ever to confront the country — his timidity over Zimbabwe, or in his dealings with the sensitive matter of race in our politics, he has made worse the disfigured nationhood bequeathed us by apartheid.

This week he has taken us across a new threshold. He has allowed the organs of state security to be deployed in defence of his leadership of the ruling party.

It is difficult to comment on President Thabo Mbeki's utterances on e.tv this week on HIV/Aids without using language that would show immense disrespect to the high office he represents, even if not to the man himself.

Asked if he would have an Aids test, Mbeki said, no, it was irrelevant and would set an example "within the context of a particular paradigm". But we're already within that paradigm, Mr President. HIV/Aids is woven into our country as intimately as the virus binds itself to the DNA of those it infects. It is affecting our economy, and across our society people of all classes and races are dying. There are persistent rumours about which eminent people have HIV — the minister of health herself has publicly said that members of her family are living with the syndrome.

Nor would it be irrelevant for Mbeki to have an HIV test. Our Anglican bishops have already underlined their claims to moral authority by going for public HIV tests. For our first citizen to do likewise would be immensely relevant, whether or not he claimed his constitutional rights to privacy and declined to reveal the results.

Mbeki's statement on e.tv sounded like someone who does not believe the link between HIV and Aids. If he really doubts it and believes that the toxicity of anti-retroviral drugs outweighs their benefits, then government policy should reflect this. Rather than appearing as Solomonic wisdom, Mbeki's equivocation on HIV/Aids, Aids tests and anti-retroviral drugs sounds like a dissident without the courage of his convictions.

Government's schizoid attitude has already — and is now — taking a terrible toll, not only among the people smitten by HIV, but also among those in government trying to combat it. The civil servant responsible for leading the battle against HIV broke down publicly and cried over her inability to get state action against the epidemic. If she resigns, another able warrior against the emergency enveloping South Africa will have been lost.

The underlying cause of Aids is HIV. No one has provided a plausible opposing paradigm. Until Mbeki can either admit it or rebut it, our advice to the president is to shut up. There is, however, little prospect that he will take our advice. It is as if he fears that to admit to an error — or to be found to have committed one — implies, for him, some kind of annihilation as a person. How else are we to explain this unreasoned obduracy?

The same pattern is evident on Zimbabwe. He has claimed the right to public silence on the merits of the situation. This is a privilege that might be allowed if his "quiet diplomacy" had been successful. Yet his diplomacy has been a singular failure. The dictatorship of Robert Mugabe gets ever more crude, brutal and idiotic; the Zimbabwean economy spirals with increasing speed towards total collapse; ordinary Zimbabweans' appeals for formative action on their crisis from their South African neighbours become ever more hopeless; and the damage to the prospects for prosperity in our own country and the region becomes ever more severe.

Asked why, then, he does not pursue a different approach — say, a more robust policy towards Mugabe — Mbeki claims that he has, indeed, criticised the Zimbabwean leader in public and that we, or media organisations, have somehow failed to hear him. His wriggling is undignified. Its purpose is, again, to avoid admitting to what is evidently, for him, the greatest calamity: to have been wrong.

Mbeki's most shameful contribution to our society over the past 22 months, though, has been his attempts to re-racialise our politics. He has taken the perversity of apartheid and sought to make of it a virtue. He tells us repeatedly that all whites hold all blacks in contempt. What he hopes to achieve by doing so, we can only guess. Whatever it is, it cannot be far from a desire to sow division where the struggle against apartheid sought to create unity, to plant the seeds of a new nation in formation.

What are more certain are the results of Mbeki's approach: black South Africans treat their white counterparts with even greater suspicion than our unhappy history might justify; whites, their capital and skills are leaving the country at an alarming rate; what Mandela made a country of hope, confident it could overcome its tremendous difficulties, Mbeki has, in just 22 months, rendered a land of fractiousness and despair.

Why? we ask. Why? We believe the answer lies in the same territory of the mind that explains the extraordinary tales of plot and counter-plot we have heard in recent weeks and months, the unsolicited denials of ambition by leading ANC figures, and the failure by brave soldiers in the struggle against apartheid to speak out now against a leader many of them now despise yet fear.

Mbeki took us across a threshold this week when he and his Minister of Safety and Security Steve Tshwete told us, in effect, that to rival Mbeki for leadership of the ANC or the presidency of the country was both traitorous and murderous. While trying to give the appearance of standing outside the fray, Mbeki appealed on e.tv on Tuesday night for those with knowledge of any plots to come forward with their evidence, while on the national broadcaster, the SABC, Tshwete, on the flimsiest of evidence, named three of Mbeki's potential rivals for leadership of the ANC as, allegedly, dangers to the president's life.

This is low, low stuff. It is the stuff of the Soviet Union under Josef Stalin, or of Malawi under Kamuzu Banda. Had the three named individuals been discussing Mbeki's replacement (and we know of no evidence that they have) this would have been entirely legitimate and the very stuff of democracy. By using words such as "plot", Mbeki and Tshwete have created notions of gunpowder and treason.

It was preceded by weeks during which we on this newspaper heard repeated stories of leaks to the SABC intended to embarrass Deputy President Jacob Zuma emanating from individuals associated with the presidency. It came barely a month after the editor of this newspaper was told by a senior official in the presidency that, if the *Mail & Guardian* carried further references to the president's sexual habits, he could expect a "personal hell".

Mathews Phosa, Cyril Ramaphosa and Tokyo Sexwale — the three named by Tshwete — are no angels. They are robust businessmen and politicians. Might we not, however, expect them also to have been accorded by the government the dignity and presumption of innocence the ANC and government have been demanding for Messrs Yengeni and others who might have benefited from the R50-billion arms deal?

The arms deal is — as we predicted it would when the ANC excluded the Heath commission from the investigation into it — haunting the ANC. And so it will continue to do for as long as the ANC and the government give the appearance of not promoting the fullest possible investigation into the scandal surrounding the self-enrichment via the deal of a number of senior individuals associated with the ruling party.

As we reveal on pages two and three of this newspaper today, under Mbeki's chairmanship the Cabinet decided in 1999 to incur what is now a R50-billion bill (and rising) for the arms deal, notwithstanding evidence before it from the Ministry of Finance that the defence purchases would seriously damage this country's ability to take the bulk of its citizens beyond poverty.

The time is long past for members of the ANC to ask themselves whether this is the kind of leadership they want, or that the country needs. A great party is at risk of being turned into the instrument of a man caught up in his own personal rages and with so brittle an ego that he fears evisceration if he retreats on an issue or allows a recognition that he has failed.

In December next year the ANC decides whether this man should continue as president of the party. It also has the power to determine substantially whether he should continue as president of the country. At least, the time has come for the ANC to conclude that the president of the ANC and of the country should not be one and the same person.

ANC members are already asking the same question as we are: Is Thabo Mbeki fit to rule? They now need to recover the courage to answer it. It does not follow that they are conspirators or murderers if they do so honestly.

April 26 2001

LETTERS

Racists masquerading as journalists

The *Mail & Guardian* asks whether President Thabo Mbeki is fit to rule. I ask: Who are these racists masquerading as newspapermen?

It is patently untrue that Mbeki has rendered South Africa a land of fractiousness and despair in just 22 months. What the *M&G* is effectively saying is that blacks should keep quiet about the racism they are subjected to because whites will then leave the country with their skills and capital at an alarming rate. An overwhelmingly high proportion of the population of this country voted Mbeki and his party into power. When and if we believe Mbeki is not fit to rule, we shall vote him and his party out of power.

The president's "sin" is to have the courage to express the feelings and frustrations of blacks in their own country. — *Chane Ketane, Faerie Glen, Pretoria; May 4 2001*

Welcome to cuckoo-land

Your neo-liberal rantings about Mbeki and the disarray in the African National Congress, besides being divisive and irresponsible, smack increasingly of Democratic Alliance propaganda. Has the *M&G* perchance sold out to Tony Leon and his cronies? By maintaining that Mbeki has attempted to re-racialise our politics, are you implying that it has ever been deracialised? If so, welcome to cuckoo-land and the grass is blue! — *Frank Kantor, Kloof; May 4 2001*

Sensational and exaggerated

I respect the *M&G* as a credible watchdog of society, but your front-page comments on Mbeki's reign are sensational and exaggerated. It is Mbeki's government that worked with civil society to challenge greedy pharmaceutical firms in court to allow poor people to have access to HIV/Aids drugs at a cheaper price.

Mbeki has come out in favour of a constructive engagement with neo-colonialism as represented by multinationals. It is the responsibility of civil society, in partnership with government, to point the way for emerging local ventures to compete or collaborate with multinational concerns.

You continue nailing Mbeki on the question of his stance on Zimbabwe's President Robert Mugabe. South Africa has a much more important role to play in the Southern African Development Community region economically than making destructive comments against the gay-bashing and blatantly racist old man from Zim.

Africa's praise poets were critical of our rulers, but they also said good thing about them. The Western media have a thing or two to learn from Africa's praise poets as custodians of the continent's oral literary tradition Balance is one of them. You can do it. Don't allow the relationship between our leaders and the media to degenerate. — *Sihle Smahla, Pietermaritzburg; May 4 2001*

No holy cow

I found the *M&G*'s editorial both daring and invigorating. Contrary to the opinion of many of my fellow comrades, I sighed with relief at the realisation that democracy is vibrant through the medium of a free press in South Africa.

The president is not a holy cow, sacrosanct or above the people. What he is facing is just one of the perils of being first citizen in a system that is not built on messianic complexes. For we do not need a president who is the embodiment of all that is holy and good — at all costs — even if that means lying to the people. What we need is honesty, integrity and the desire to debate the truth.

Criticising leadership is by no means equivalent to criticising "black" leaders. In fact, it is the very kind of obsequious reverence for a leader (simply because he has your pigmentation) that is the very bedrock of racially motivated leadership.

South Africans deserve the best. The struggle against apartheid was an enormous feat involving great minds, great strategists, great souls and great loss of blood. But democracy is not won overnight. It is good to keep up the struggle for justice and valid non-racialism.

When I lived in Kenya in 1995 I saw that every radio broadcast began with "President Daniel arap Moi today said that ..." and every office or cafè had to have a picture of the president in it. Africa's history of megalomaniacal and self-important leaders (not withstanding their colonial predecessors' example) reveals important lessons of the dangers of presidentialism. Instead of growth, repression, corruption and brutality flourish.

Of course none of us can as yet say who the next president should or will be. However, I wish to suggest that the people elect him or her by popular vote, rather than having an ANC caucus or cabal enforce such a decision. — *Khetiwe Khanya, Pietermaritzburg; May 4 2001*

Smelly red herrings

Is there any plot at all? Is this not a ploy to distract us from the arms-buying scandal? Were the never-ending revelations on the activities of the Xhosa mafia becoming too much for the mob? More likely Tokyo's trio were not big fish at all but just simply smelly red herrings. — *Should I Pack for Perth? May 4 2001*

Disillusioned would-be revolutionaries

You state that Mbeki's most shameful contribution to our society is his attempt to "re-racialise" our politics by "telling us repeatedly that all whites hold all blacks in contempt". When was this era you hark back to of deracialised politics? Now if you were talking about the role played by the DA here, I might understand it.

The notion that the ANC under Mbeki is responsible for the racialisation of politics is one that has gained currency among a particular group of people — a group who, in their arrogance, believe that this view is shared by all within the country — a group who perceive themselves as the new victims in what is (as people may need reminding) a democracy.

We have in place in this country extraordinary systems, principles and institutions that guard us against excesses of power. Is the assumption you make that all these are rendered useless and incompetent in the face of the enormous power wielded by one man? Or is the assumption that because we are an African country the population is just too slow-witted to properly implement democracy?

When you ask the plaintive question "Why, we ask, why?" you come to the conclusion that the answer lies in "the territory of the mind". If I may be so bold, the question needs to be turned inward and the answer may well be the same. Why, Mr Barrell, why? Just as reformed alcoholics and smokers make for the most effective and vitriolic campaigners against these habits, how true is this of disillusioned would-be revolutionaries?

The *M&G* has a long and proud history as an independent and critical newspaper. From what I remember it also has a long and proud history as a newspaper that subscribed to broad-based principles of the profession of journalism: these would include accuracy, honesty, fairness and responsibility. What's happened? — *Paula McBride; May 4 2001*

Rather the devil you know

I agree that there has been a series of unmitigated disasters surrounding Mbeki's presidency. But there is another side to his leadership: economically, the country has never been in better shape. Inflation is down, our external reserves are growing, the budget deficit is decreasing, and so on. Arms deals aside, the government appears to be building an economic base that conceivably holds the key to long-term development and social upliftment.

It is understandable that people want to fast-track social upliftment. But it is a stable economy that ensures its sustainability in the long term. Let's not kid ourselves. South Africa is trying to recover from 350 years of economic exploitation, both internally by the privileged classes and externally by colonial powers. That is not going to be fixed in a single presidential term.

I fear that replacing the president could destroy everything achieved so far. There are many opponents to the present government's economic policies in the ANC — the trade union movements and the South African Communist Party — and there is a real possibility that rivals might engage in Mugabesque behaviour where long-term vision is traded for short-term political power.

Let's not call for new leaders unless we have a clear idea of who the next will be. Rather the devil you know than the devil you don't. — *Devil's Advocate; May 4 2001*

I confess ...

It is with the deepest and most profound regret that I write to inform you that the conspiracy to oust Mbeki is not limited to Cdes Mathews Phosa, Cyril Ramaphosa and Tokyo Sexwale. For I too, I shudder to mention, have been a part of that selfsame conspiracy.

Indeed, I make bold to say, it is a conspiracy of international proportions and utterly diabolical depravity. We have, I take courage to counsel, operatives strategically located in all the major capitals of the world. These *agents provocateurs* shamefully influence the international media corporations to disgorge the most bitter anti-Mbeki propaganda imaginable.

I myself, I enact fortitude to affirm, have paid vast sums to US newspapers to propagate the genocidal myth that HIV causes Aids. These funds were made available to me by a mysterious businessman with links to a nefarious syndicate of formerly communist international bankers known only as "The Counter-Renaissance".

For my own involvement in this underworld intrigue, I adopt remorsefully to recant. Had it not been for your gallant declaration of resistance to this sedition, who knows how I may yet have sullied my soul.

I have the honour to remain, Sir, your most obedient and humble servant. — *SJP May, Stanford University, California; May 4 2001*

May God forgive you, President Mbeki

It's time we talked out about what is happening to our country. The president seems to be busy playing word games with foreigners while our children and young people are drying up and dying like beautiful cut flowers in a vase. We all know it. There is no family now that has escaped this HIV/Aids scourge. It is our shame.

In our homes, young people who should be graduating from university are lying in bed dying. Little ones who should be running strong and healthy are lying on blankets, already corpses. We don't talk about it. The president says he cannot afford drugs, not even enough to save some of our unborn children from this plague from hell — even though we are told some of these drugs are free or only R21. He tells us it is too complicated for us. The drugs might not be safe. The scientists don't understand. It's poverty, it's tuberculosis, our people wouldn't know how to use powdered milk, it's this, and this, and this.

The president says he is busy fighting racism. But the racists are laughing their heads off at us, our leaders talking and talking with fools while we make our undertakers rich burying more of our children every week than PW Botha ever dreamed of killing.

Thabo Mbeki is too proud to admit he was wrong about this HIV thing. Pride is a sign of a weak leader. In hard times like these a people needs a strong and humble leader. Mbeki, if you want to be a world leader, go to the United Nations. Let us find a president who cares about his own people. Let us have a leader who will mobilise the whole country and all its resources to fight this curse like lions.

Mbeki, even if the people are not well-informed about what you are doing now, history and God are watching you. For every African child that could have been saved, for every family's rivers of grief that should have been tears of joy, while you stood idle, may God in his mercy forgive you.
— *PS Dlamini, Lamontville, Durban; September 15 2001*

Is South Africa brain dead?

David Beresford

The weekend was quite spoilt for me by the sudden apprehension that South Africa might be brain dead. That the body is kept alive for sentimental reasons by well-intentioned medics, functioning with the help of bits and pieces of machinery. But that the professionals attendant on the body would, if polled, give as their considered opinion that the patient is no longer capable of conscious thought.

This was clearly a panic attack and I'm not sure whether I should be writing about it at all. Perhaps I should swallow a pill. It is all very well discussing the state of mind of the president in the public prints, but speculation whether a country should be pronounced dead seems somehow to be taking things a bit far.

But I raise the question more in the hope of gaining reassurance than of pronouncing the obsequies. No one would be happier than I if the patient gave a surreptitious wink, to signal that all is well and a well-earned rest is being enjoyed. It would even be a relief if the suspected corpse would rise up and deliver a withering denunciation of me for the effrontery of spreading rumours about its premature demise.

The basis of the fear is not scientific. It is more a case of a relative wandering unattended into an intensive care unit and being alarmed at the sound of beeping and the sight of a flat line on a monitor situated next to a much-loved one's head.

The alarm in this case took the form of a story that appeared in the *Sunday Times* the weekend before last, headed: "Man poses as Mbeki's 'secret agent'". It began with a startling account of how the National Intelligence Agency (NIA) — South Africa's counterpart to the CIA, or MI5 — instructed "presidential staff to keep away from a man who, they say, has for five years masqueraded as a secret agent reporting directly to the president, Thabo Mbeki".

Now, self-evidently, this fascinating tale — attributed to senior sources in the presidency and the NIA — gave rise to problems for the reader, quite apart from those arising for the president. In particular, it presented ambiguities with regard to masquerading. Was the charge one levelled against a secret agent pretending to be an adviser to the president, or against a presidential adviser impersonating a secret agent?

Reading on did not help. In fact, it confused the plot further when it emerged that, during the five years "the man" had ambiguously served the president, the presidency had neglected to ascertain his true identity. "The man", it transpired from the *Sunday Times* story (based, as said earlier, on presidential and intelligence sources), was known to the president's staff as Bheki Jacobs. But he held himself out to the newspaper, in what appeared to have been an otherwise uninformative interview, to be one Uranian Solomons. The newspaper added, authoritatively, that he was also known to masquerade as Vladimir Illich Solomons, Hassan Solomons and, on occasion, "King" Solomon Solomons.

The report went on to denounce this mysterious character as the trouble-maker behind a number of recent controversies that had embarrassed the president. He was said to have circulated allegations such as those of government corruption in a multibillion-rand arms deal, claims of big-business involvement in a planned party coup and other gossip doing the rounds with regard to the head of state.

It was, self-evidently, a major political story, if one that raised more questions than it answered. But answers would surely follow. The president would, I reasoned to myself, summon a press conference on the Monday, either to denounce the report as a monstrous fabrication or to confirm it. If to confirm it, then to announce at the very least a judicial commission of inquiry to establish how an unidentified man had managed to pass himself off to the head of state for five years, whether as a bogus presidential adviser or a fake secret agent. After all, if such confusion is apparent on the bridge of the ship of state, are the passengers and the crew not entitled to reassurance that someone, preferably qualified, has a hand on the helm?

The anticipated controversy failed to materialise last week. On Sunday, hoping for clarification one way or another, I rushed out to buy the *Sunday Times* again. "'Secret agent' sowed fear and loathing", announced the headline to the story on page two. But the report underneath added little more by way of substantive information, other than to announce the man's "real name is Hassan Solomons". How they know that is difficult to fathom since the report goes on to disclose that the Department of Home Affairs — presumably due authority where identity is concerned in this country — has him registered as Uranian Vladimir Dzerzhinsky Joseph Solomons.

It was as I put aside the newspaper that the morbid thought hit me as to the functioning of South Africa's brain. It struck me that this story and others like it — ranging across the entire spectrum of what is properly subject for public scandal, from the gang rape and death of Chris Hani's daughter, to the Helena Dolny affair, to the refusal of authority to release crime statistics — are pin-pricks to the body politic.

As when a neurologist sticks a needle into the limbs in search of evidence as to the proper functioning of the nervous system, so such stories demand a certain reflex reaction by society. When limb after limb is jabbed and fails to provide the due response, it is perhaps time to take several deep breaths and say as calmly as possible to the nearest stethoscope: "Ah ... excuse me venturing a suggestion, being totally unqualified in this area, but could the patient be, well, you know, be ... ?"

March 23 2001

Give us a good reason to vote

Glenda Daniels

I spent last weekend agonising about whether to vote in the local government elections. As a black South African, how can one not vote after so many people have made sacrifices, suffered enormous hardship and even died to make a democratic South Africa possible? From this point of view the very thought of not exercising one's newly won right to vote seems ludicrously irresponsible.

But to vote you need to have a level of confidence in the party you're voting for. And not to vote indicates a lack of commitment to the country, and shows no civic duty and responsibility. I've often heard journalists declare that they won't vote because, loftily, they believe they are already making an equally important contribution by covering elections. Also, they would prefer to be non-partisan so that they can be "fair", the argument goes.

I joined the African National Congress at the age of 19 after I'd finished "A" levels in Botswana, and even though I haven't been an active member since I became a journalist more than 10 years ago, I have been a loyal but sometimes critical supporter. I've become more critical with every year, and am now disillusioned.

After returning to South Africa in 1984 I became a T-shirt-wearing, flag-waving, toyi-toying activist in many mass democratic structures such as the United Democratic Front, the Azanian Students' Organisation, the South African Students Congress, the Natal Indian Congress, and the ANC Youth League. In these organisations I was committed to and optimistic about the future of a country where racial tensions would ease and poverty and sexism would be at least alleviated.

Now I find myself feeling politically alienated because I disagree on fundamental issues of principle on far too many of the ANC's stances. These issues have been raised *ad nauseam* by this newspaper. And, interestingly enough, I've heard many old comrades and party faithfuls, after a few glasses of wine at a dinner party, shyly and reluctantly agreeing with the *Mail & Guardian* on its criticisms of the president's and the government's incessant and unhelpful muddying of the water concerning the link between HIV and Aids.

This agreement extends to the *M&G*'s critiques of the government's stance on Zimbabwe — particularly its refusal to condemn manifest human rights abuses there. And the too often unfortunately Africanist views on race emanating from officialdom come under dinner-party fire too. Not the whole of the ANC shares these views, but if the president is espousing them, then the party is tainted and so is the government.

It's a long time since I've heard anything along the lines of: "We are all South Africans, we have to assert our nationhood and not think of ourselves as black or white, but rather work towards making a better future for all." The non-racial ideal seems to have disappeared since we all stood in long queues to vote, for the first time democratically, in 1994. Many say it disappeared with the end of Nelson Mandela's reign. Maybe, but what I find unfortunate is this: when, as a black person, one says Mandela was a great president, a lot of fellow black journalists and friends look at you askance as if to say, "You might as well be a white liberal" — because their view is often that Mbeki gets criticised because "he is a strong black president who is not kowtowing to white fears and needs, as Mandela did".

Well, I think that is all nonsense. It's time to forget defending people because they are black or white or any race, but rather look at what we need right now, and that is for someone at the top to unite this country, which seems to be currently nationally depressed. The national depression is not just among the chattering classes (I think journalists fall into this category too), but also among township people who live in shacks and are often unemployed, workers on farms whose lives have not changed or petrol-pump attendants who earn measly wages.

I'm not saying let's stop talking about race issues, or that they don't exist: talk about it all you like, if it makes you happy. But let's rather look at real issues instead of using race to deflect attention from weaknesses. I saw an outstandingly outrageous example of this at the Congress of South African Trade Unions (Cosatu) conference last month — which was so brilliantly organised, by the way, that I think Cosatu should take a shot at running the country.

At the congress, Mbeki cunningly avoided real tensions between labour and the government by making a speech about how the racist opposition is "trying to divide our people". Many Cosatu delegates were startled and puzzled. They wanted, after all, a response to issues in the alliance such as macroeconomic policy, among others. In fact, during the lunch break, after Mbeki had spoken, many delegates said that it was a "clever" speech as it did not deal with the workers.

But back to voting. In my view the Democratic Alliance is a party to protect white privilege, so I couldn't possibly vote for them. I sometimes wonder what whites who previously voted for the Democratic Party will now do. I don't think many previous DP supporters will with a clear conscience be able to vote for the DA. So liberals are feeling alienated too, even though it no doubt lifts their heavy hearts when they see television images of Tony Leon schmoozing up to black people in Soweto, and even trying to toyi-toyi.

If I were a liberal rather than a left-leaning person, then I still wouldn't have a party to vote for. We need another party, one that will stick with true non-racialism and will happily house all those people whom I have a lot in common with — black and white, rich and poor, men and women, feminists, trade unionists, environmentalists, gay rights activists, Aids activists, anti-gun lobbyists ...

In the meanwhile, we don't have that other party, so I can't vote. But maybe the ANC will take up the challenge from thousands of politically alienated people and get back to its original principles. We can still dream, can't we?

October 27 2000

Use your vote to fight a one-party state

Rhoda Kadalie

Glenda Daniels captures very eloquently the sentiments of people on the left about voting for the African National Congress in the next election ("Give us a good reason to vote"). But I wish to suggest that Daniels's view, and it is the view of many on the left, is deeply flawed and highly problematic for the development of democracy in South Africa. It is based on a sentimentalism and nostalgia for the sense of common purpose that characterised the liberation movement.

Our common purpose was to overthrow apartheid, and nothing more, even though we in the liberation movement assumed common interests across class, race, ethnicity, gender and so on. The post-apartheid era has demonstrated very vividly that even people on the left (former comrades) had very little in common with each other, as fights soon broke out among comrades in the Independent Broadcasting Authority (IBA), the Human Rights Commission, the SABC, the Land Bank and the ANC.

Many of my friends admit that they have lost political perspective because of their loyalty to the ANC. Loyalty to the party has taken precedence over loyalty to justice. As a liberation movement, the ANC had the moral high ground. As the majority party in government it no longer commands that moral high ground and can be found wanting on many levels, because it has reneged on many of its own very noble policies.

The challenge is to grow and consolidate democracy in South Africa by looking very closely at other post-independence countries in Africa, Latin America and Eastern Europe. And this requires respect from both government and civil society for the development of a democratic culture that, at times, requires precedence over party loyalties.

Unfortunately the donor community withdrew a lot of their funding from NGOs after 1994, preferring to pump money into government, weakening civil society quite dramatically after 1994. There is an acknowledgement that this was the wrong decision, and attempts are being made to redress this situation.

The culture of political correctness has also contributed very seriously to the silence of civic organisations that did not want to be seen criticising a democratic government and a black one at that. In addition to this silence was a failure to reposition themselves strategically vis-a-vis the new state. Instead of being proactive and assisting the government with delivery and developing capacity, the NGOs react to government failures smugly.

A vibrant multiparty democracy needs a multiplicity of voices, and Tim Modise's radio programme, *The Tim Modise Show,* is an example of how one grows tolerance and respect for a diversity of views. Patricia de Lille has played a crucial role in holding the government accountable on the arms deal, children in detention, Aids and so on. The proliferation of one-party states in Africa demonstrates the importance of encouraging multi-party views, however unpalatable some of them are. Respect for the concept of loyal opposition is a very alien concept in post-independence countries in general and in the ANC in particular!

The Aids debacle and the conference on racism in the media are indications that internal democracy is not alive and well in the ANC. Opposition parties, too, can be loyal to democracy, even should they differ on matters of policy. To dismiss them by constantly racialising them is to fail to assess them on merit. Developing opposition requires that we look past race and look at how opposition as an institution needs to be cultivated and developed.

It is customary for the left, after independence, to dismiss opposition and wait for the fateful day until a social democratic/socialist movement is formed to oppose the new government in power. And what happens when nobody is looking is that people vote again and again for the ANC, for sentimental reasons, entrenching their majority and so eroding the possibility of a real opposition developing.

The all-inclusive opposition that Daniels is looking for only happens in 20 years' time, as in Zimbabwe, when it is far too late. There is a growing alliance between the trade union movement, the South African Communist Party and the South African National NGO Coalition. No real democratic centre is developing that will keep the country on track in terms of its accountability to the citizens; hence the proliferation of litigation on issues of socio-economic rights.

The public will increasingly use the Constitutional Court to challenge the non-delivery of services to the public. The Grootboom community housing case, the Aids lobby, pensions by the Black Sash, are examples of how people are going to use other institutions to hold the government accountable as they increasingly lose faith in the government to prioritise their concerns. Social and political scientists have studied this for years and, true to form, this is what happens in most post-independence countries, to the detriment of the development of truly democratic states.

The role of Parliament is steadily being marginalised as decision-making shifts more and more to the executive. Question time has been restricted and increasingly Parliament has become a rubber stamp for the government, as exemplified by its support for the presidential view on Aids, the serving of subpoenas on media editors, the Zimbabwe issue, Minister of Justice and Constitutional Development Penuell Maduna's utterances and so on.

MPs are not engaging with issues as they should. They seem to be more on recess than in office, except for a few. They key question is how parliamentary oversight should interact with executive authority. To quote a Centre for Development and Enterprise report: "This unfortunate disjuncture between Members of Parliament and voters weakens MPs within their parties and in Parliament as a whole. It adds to a feeling of isolation between 'leaders and the led' and strengthens the hand of the party leadership."

But just recently we had a brief glimpse of what Parliament could be like with the public disciplining of an MP. But he is a small fry, so it is easy to make a public example of him. What about Winnie Mandela, Maduna and many others who have not been called to order? The public accounts standing committee's handling of the arms deal is another good example. It is rare that an ANC MP challenges the executive on its performance or lack of it.

Due to its dominance in Parliament, the ANC dominates the committee system, and even outvotes the opposition wherever it can. Yet many ANC MPs are reluctant to use their powers to hold the executive accountable.

It is easy to expose soft targets, and not those within the ranks. The two-thirds majority is therefore detrimental to growing a vibrant democracy. Furthermore, the independence of the media should be guarded at all costs. The persecution of the media under the guise of the accusation of racism was a blatant attempt to control it, as it was to undermine it, and the Human Rights Commission acted as a willing agent to carry out the government's agenda sideways. By racialising the media, the government has been consistently guilty of trying to weaken them.

Then there are those journalists and editors who have given their fair share in contributing to compromising media independence — by becoming the mouthpiece of the government, by avoiding criticism of the government and by suffering from the disease of political correctness because of white guilt. The recent Shaun Johnson fiasco over free advertising given to the government is a case in point.

Independent media institutions such as the IBA, the SABC, and even certain editors have been complicit in eroding the freedom and independence of the press because of white guilt.

In conclusion, a two-thirds majority government is detrimental to democracy in South Africa, because then Parliament and government are very much one and the same thing. Everybody is shocked about the arms deal, which seems to be escalating by the millions the deeper the investigation goes. We constantly hear that there is no money to address issues of national concern, but then there is money for a 15% increase, above the inflation rate, to MPs and ministers; R78-million has been found to revamp the civic centre for the Cape Town Unicity. Money was found to put together an Aids Council that was not needed. Money was found to mount a racism conference in Sandton. We have been rocked by our fair share of corruption scandals and in many instances the money has still not been recovered.

I am convinced that there is enough money to do what is doable, but somehow we have failed to hold government accountable. For all the money that has been wasted, Crossroads and Alexandra, by now, could have been redeveloped to give hope to the poor. The poor clearly are not the government's priority. The solution is to challenge and decrease the ANC's majority in the local government election, as a majority government is not good for any democracy.

November 10 2000

The presidency disappears up its own fundament

Robert Kirby

Using the African National Congress website as his medium, President Thabo Mbeki recently published some impressions of South Africa he acquired from a visiting Martian lady. He revealed these in a melancholy *Letter from the President* headed "Clamour over Zimbabwe reveals continuing racial prejudice in SA".

While Mbeki was giving his Martian lady visitor a guided tour round South African white racial prejudice, the Venusian pilot of the flying saucer in which she had travelled had some time on his hands. Hovering over the Union Buildings he was able to use the spacecraft's very advanced technology to have his own look into the secret workings of the South African presidency itself.

What first impressed the Venusian pilot was the sheer efficiency of the presidency staff. Many in number, the compass of their duties was, however, severely restricted. But they applied themselves to their chores with diligence and commitment. Closer inspection of the hard drives of their amusingly rudimentary computers revealed that the secret of the presidency's efficiency was, indeed, its utter simplicity. More than eight-tenths of the total drive-space was occupied with a stupendous array of description, argument, analysis, research, comment, review, deconstruction, contemplation and reflection, all on a single theme: a somewhat bitter abstraction called "race".

This single, small word was apparently the humble cornerstone of an immense and complex cognitive structure. From his knowledge of primitive worship formalities the pilot recognised the presidency for what it was: an intellectual cathedral for worship of the oldest religious precept in the galactic system: Holy Victimology.

The Venusian pilot watched in wonder as at regular intervals an office buzzer would sound and the loyal acolytes in the presidency would bow down, touch their speaking organs to the floor and raise their voices in joyful worship of Holy Victimology. They would be led in these prayer rites by their team leader, a vast and jovial wild-haired fellow referred to affectionately behind his back as The First Enema.

Once prayers were over the staff would fall to yet more pious onslaught of their computers, inventing staggering new variations on the central theme. They hammered out endless stodgy dissertations on the subject, subdividing it into arcane sub-specialities like "Naked Racism among White Oyster-Sexers", "Colour Bigotry Destroys Soccer Plans", "Rich Whites Plan SuperCity to Exclude Poor Blacks", "Zimbabwe: A Victim of White Colonial Greed", "When Democracy Triumphs Who Gives a Purple Shit How Many Elderly Farm Couples are Raped and Bludgeoned?" and "Keeping the Struggle Alive by Naming Abject Squatter Settlements After Political Heroes". The variations were endless and in their brilliant circuits was revealed a creative imagination of stellar proportions.

Chewing on his ammonia-flavoured nutrition bar the Venusian pilot pondered on what he had found when scanning these writings, listened in to the frenzied discussions of the presidency staff. They fair brimmed with terms like "moral" and "constitutional" and "scrupulous" and "a better life for all" and many other tentacle-warming symbologies. The only thing that seemed to interrupt the presidency's steady quotidian rhythm were occasional, brief visits by its leader, President Thabo the Selfless, who dropped by to tell them how heartbroken he had felt when looking down from his luxury R300-million jet airliner on the wretched victims of something called apartheid. "People are living in cardboard hovels, feeding off rubbish dumps," he would proclaim sadly. "I had to forcibly stop myself throwing them down some smoked salmon sandwiches."

After consulting with his inner self the Venusian came to the conclusion that the South African presidency was actually a working model of the intergalactic phenomenon termed rather enticingly a black hole in space. The presidency staff will probably be distressed to learn that being likened to a black hole in space has nothing whatsoever to do with racism. Black holes are so called because no light escapes a collapsing star as it disappears up its own fundament.

It was in the deployment of this latter talent that the presidency staff seemed at their most efficient. After a recent racism conference, attended by the entire presidency staff, four of their members could not be found. All they discovered were some badly singed sphincters from which no light could be seen escaping.

As he warmed up his engines for the return flight the Venusian pilot made concise notes in his ship's log, knowing these would be of considerable interest to solar anthropologists on his home planet. Nothing particularly new, he noted.

All they need urgently is another few centuries and a far less pathetic website.

April 6 2001

Pour on the gravy

Rather than buying a luxury jet for R300-million, has the government considered air-freighting part of our world-famous Blue Train for those important trips for our VIPs?

Each carriage takes eight passengers in great style and comfort, and the economics make sense: three carriages at 40 tons each = 120 tons. Freight cost: R1 000 a ton per 1 000km. For an average-distance flight into sub-Saharan Africa, look at a round-trip distance of 8 000km, at R960 000 a trip. Add another R500 000 a trip to hire the carriages and get them into and out of the freight plane. This gives a cost of about R1,5-million a trip.

Investing R300-million at 10% gives R30-million a year, enough for 20 trips annually. — *Gravy enthusiast, Cowies Hill; March 23 2001*

Let them eat salmon

Thuli Nhlapo

It was raining last weekend when the Greater East Rand Metro mayor Bamvumile Vilakazi was inaugurated at a glamorous celebration at the Kopanong hotel in Benoni. In African culture, they say the rain signals blessings from happy ancestors.

Because his name is Bamvumile ("they have agreed"), it could be assumed everybody at the council, renamed the Ekurhuleni Metropolitan Council (the Tsonga name means "the place of peace"), agreed to spend R400 000 on the party.

Traffic officers directed guests to the parking bays at the hotel. One luxury car after another pulled into the hotel, offloading mainly African National Congress officials. Ordinary residents of Ekurhuleni were bused to Barnard stadium in Kempton Park earlier in the day for their part of the celebration.

As the rain sobbed heavily down, one could not help but think of squatters in nearby Thokoza whose homes were demolished by the council just a few days earlier. In the shivering night air, the little glasses of what smelled like extremely expensive whisky being offered to guests arriving at the banquet would perhaps have warmed several fingers and toes in Thokoza.

This was no cheap suit and A-line black dress affair — the room was ripe for the society pages. With so-called traditional dress *de rigueur* at nearly every function these days, the room was peppered liberally with modern touched-up Xhosa, Ndebele and Venda dress, and the occasional sari. The tell-tale thickened edges around the hems indicated that many a dress was hot off the dressmaker's machine.

A diamond bracelet here and a Fendi bag there ensured that no improper connections would be made between the wearers and the less sophisticated. Female guests stood around, not too far from the lone photographer, just in case he wanted their image for a newspaper. Only one enterprising husband, sporting a shirt that matched his wife's dress, was in any form of traditional dress; the rest were in dark suits.

Waiting for the mayor to arrive was almost like waiting at a church for a bride in a wedding ceremony. And like a bride, he did not disappoint: an entourage of eight Benoni central policing unit cars ushered the mayor and the mayoress to their celebration of themselves. The cars had to stop right before the entrance, perhaps to protect the couple from being soaked like the squatters down the road.

A short man with a pot-belly first came into the banquet hall to inspect the room before the mayor could walk in. That was the chief bodyguard. Seven more clean-shaven men in long designer jackets and square-toed shoes followed. Those were also bodyguards. Even though the mayor of Tshwane, Father Smangaliso Mkhatshwa, former Gauteng premier Mathole Motshekga and Minister of Arts, Culture, Science and Technology Ben Ngubane were already helping themselves to starters in the banquet room — with no bodyguards — Vilakazi was whisked away to a special room. He could not have been polishing his long, boring speech in the special room because waitresses came in and out with bottles of wine and plates of smoked salmon.

After what seemed like a century, the mayor emerged, still surrounded by bored bodyguards who kept themselves busy by pushing people out of the way of their charge. Vilakazi's speech was about "people-centred and developmental local government", but he forgot to mention that more than 500 Thokoza Unit F residents had their shacks bulldozed and their belongings taken away by the private security company Wozani.

His guests applauded when the mayor said he stopped inhumane and insensitive acts "like cutting electricity for our people" in the place of peace. Because the mayor's speech was long and predictable, and because there was plenty of free booze, a drunk man sitting at table 25 with Motshekga spoke out loudly about "them saying one thing every time".

If the sour cream and salmon starter did not leave a bitter taste in the mouth, an altercation during the mayor's speech would have done it. When a lone, red-faced white man, obviously drunk, began making rather disparaging remarks — to himself, but loudly — about the charismatically challenged speech, the bodyguards, standing at the back of the hall, moved in.

In a manoeuvre reminiscent of an American testosterone movie, in one quick swoop they surrounded the man, swivelled his chair around and yanked him out of the room. In the reception lobby there were strong racial undertones as the man was shoved around by the bodyguards — to the delight of a nearby photographer, who was happily snapping away. This agitated one of the heavies, who threatened to confiscate his film. Eventually, the man was sent sprawling on to the marble floor, landing near the potato salad and chicken livers.

The mayor must love parties — this was his second inaugural ceremony. He had a party in December, but a representative of the council said the catered affair was "a normal practice for a council meeting". The Democratic Alliance boycotted the party on Friday, saying Ekurhuleni's finance committee had already proposed to borrow R100-million, of which R26-million would cover its operating deficit.

The mayor has not yet restored peace to the place of peace. Residents at the informal settlement are still waiting to get their belongings back. While the mayor was protected from the rain, the "poor people" he kept on referring to in his speech were waiting for a good Samaritan to donate tents to them because they are still homeless.

March 2 2001

The children of fire

Khadija Magardie

The smell of burning human flesh is one of the most unpleasant on earth. Caregivers and emergency workers say that the very first whiff mystifyingly brings on palpitations. And the faintly musty, sourish odour is not easily forgotten: it tends to linger in the nostrils — for days.

Imagine having to live with that smell every day, because looking in the mirror somehow encourages your senses to produce the smell in your nostrils. Imagine searing pain all over your body, especially your face and hands — a fierce burning that makes you want to dive into water to make it go away, but you are being restrained, so you cannot run. Imagine a room full of strange people in green gowns and big masks bending over you shouting instructions.

You wake up later, groggy, in a bed with white sheets. You cannot feel your face because there are just swollen, blistered lumps where your hands used to be. You scream for your mother, but nobody is there, only people who look like they have plastic over their faces, who walk by your cot occasionally. You fall asleep and when you wake up again two nurses are lowering you on to a plastic bed, where they start unwrapping the bandages around your head and those limbs you can still recognise as legs and arms. With each touch, you scream wildly, as the burning returns again. The little pieces falling off the bandage are your own skin.

After what seems like a lifetime of the same routine — sleeping, waking up, sleeping, waking up — a strange person comes to collect you from your cot. They say you are leaving the place where you have been feeling all this pain and going somewhere with this person. Nobody tells you where your mother is; in fact, the nurses appear too frightened to look you in the eye every time you ask for her. But you are just happy to leave that place where they have been hurting you for so many months.

This can all be pretty scary if you are only five years old. When you arrive at the place the stranger takes you to, you are given a little room with its own little bed. Next to the bed is a dressing table, with a stool and a mirror. Even though it's difficult to walk and you still feel tender, you walk over to the mirror and look at yourself. And instantly, you wish with all your heart you were back in the hospital ...

There are places in South Africa that the rest of the country would prefer not to know about. These are the paediatric burn units that care for the countless numbers of infants, toddlers and children who are burned, some beyond recognition, by everyday items.

Hot water is one. In the suburbs, where there are well-protected bathtubs, taps that normally run tepid water from modern geysers and always someone on hand in case of an accident, it is unlikely that a child could lose a limb, or a life, from hot water burns. But in a one-bedroom shack in an informal settlement, with no electricity or running water, an adult preparing to bathe a child may first pour stove-boiled water into the tin bathtub on the floor and momentarily turn her back to refill the bucket with cold water. In that split second, the unknowing child steps into that tin bathtub, changing his or her life — if not losing it.

Burns are forever, say the brightly coloured educational posters of the

Burn Treatment Centre at Chris Hani Baragwanath hospital. Not only do they have severe physical consequences for a victim — especially a child whose body is still small, leaving little space for skin grafts — but they also leave a lasting psychological trauma that comes with not looking "acceptable" anymore. Experts say the emotional trauma of scarring and other deformities lasts for life. In a society that is unforgiving and harsh on physically disfigured people, some choose to hide away.

In many instances, parents hide children from society — not uncommon in rural, often deeply superstitious communities. But it happens also in urban areas. One badly disfigured little girl sent a Gauteng delivery man fleeing in terror over the garden gate, screaming "tokoloshe". Up to 58% of burn-injured patients display typical symptoms of mild to severe depression. Some take their own lives.

What is also spoken of in hushed tones, and whispered in hospital corridors between social workers, are the deliberate injuries inflicted on children by those nearest and dearest to them. Sizwe Ndlovu (not his real name) was only six years old when he was dragged out of a raging fire in his mother's home in a rural village about 40km outside Newcastle, KwaZulu-Natal, last year. Even the most optimistic reconstructive surgeons say the little boy's face, which was melted by the licking flames, will never look "normal" again. Sizwe nearly died in a fire set by his father, who wanted to "show" his mother for daring to claim maintenance from him for his child.

There are children whose parents burn them to punish them: placing chubby toddler hands on hot plates is a common method. Other children, especially those who are handicapped, are victims of unintentional and deliberate neglect in children's homes. Earlier this week a quadruplegic boy, in a Bloemfontein school mandated to care for him, burned to death in a shower when he was left unattended and could not turn off the hot taps.

The paediatric burn unit at Chris Hani Baragwanath hospital is one of the best in the country. It is in this unit that one sees the true face of poverty. The unit is particularly full during the winter months, when families burn fuel to keep themselves warm. Paraffin stoves, open fires, candles and cups of boiling tea are the most common culprits.

In one bed is a baby, scarcely 11 months old, who has severe burns on her abdomen — she pulled on a table cloth, and the boiling liquids on the table poured over her. A little boy, in the section for the older children, has a mangled piece of flesh, bandaged in a plastic-looking gauze, where his hand used to be. A common form of recreation in areas around squatter camps is for little boys to make boomerangs out of pieces of wire, toss them into the overhead electricity pylons and wait below to catch them.

His friend, who smiles shyly from his cot, lived in a children's home. Nearly his entire body was burned as a result of a hot water bath. Only his hands remain unhurt, and as a result, unscarred. The nurses say they were told that the child mistakenly sat in the water. But, they say, the lack of burns on his hands indicates that it was almost certain that someone was holding the boy's hands, firmly, as he boiled in the bath.

Joe Slovo squatter camp, a sprawling settlement between the suburbs of Crosby and Mayfair in Johannesburg, is one of countless others that has felt the full effects of an unstoppable fire. The sole fire hydrant — its bright yellow gleaming in the early morning light — stands in front of a home in a Crosby street, several kilometres from the entrance to the camp. Two weeks ago a fire nearly devastated the camp. Although it started in a small section of the settlement, it spread rapidly, and when the flames had died down the remains of some 160 shacks lay smouldering.

In a squatter camp, homes are in such close proximity to each other that it is nearly impossible to halt the spread of a fire. Coupled with this, many homes are constructed with highly flammable materials, such as chipboard, and in the winter months insulated with cardboard to keep warm. Inside a typical one-room shack, where there is scant space to walk around, it is easy for a paraffin stove, even a candle, to be knocked over by mistake. And whereas an adult may run for the nearest exit, or roll into some blankets to extinguish the flames, a child's first reaction is to panic.

"Too many lives are lost because people do not know what they should do in the case of a fire," says Bronwen Jones, a British journalist who founded Children of Fire, a charity dedicated to helping children who have been burned in fires and securing their access to the best medical treatment and facilities. Jones's organisation, after months of repeated haggling with the informal "landlords" and other heavies of the Joe Slovo camp, built the first firebreak in the camp. It's not much to look at — just a simple piece of land, with no grass, between two shacks in the camp. But in a shack fire — like the near-fatal one in the camp last year — a space between the flames can be a matter of life and death for the residents.

Many parents and caregivers are unaware that reconstructive surgery is available at the state's expense. And some doctors in the private sector offer their services on a *pro bono* basis. But reconstructive surgery is an extremely complicated, costly procedure that depends on racing against the clock. The longer burn injuries remain unattended, the slimmer the chance of performing effective.

One of the conditions hardest to fix is keloiding — a condition to which burnt skin is particularly susceptible. It occurs when tough, fibrous tissue forms at the site of a scar or injury. Unless operated on very early, it is nearly impossible to remedy. Zipho Zwane was burned in a fire in his family's homestead when he was only one month old. The 13-year-old from Madazane near Ladysmith, KwaZulu-Natal, is scarred on one half of his face. He has no hair on the burnt side of his face and there is only a hole where his ear used to be. His left hand is also nothing more than a swollen claw — it is common for the fingers to "melt" into each other under extreme heat.

The doctors who initially treated the boy did a mediocre job on Zipho, either because they lacked appropriate facilities or because they knew that the family would not question them. Until Zipho met Jones and came into contact with Children of Fire, he was resigned to life with his disability. But now he will receive surgery at one of Gauteng's state hospitals, under the knife of a highly skilled plastic surgeon. Titanium implants will construct his ear, and highly specialised "tissue expanders" will be inserted under his hairline: surgeons will use these to spread out his remaining hair and recreate the appearance of "normality" for the youngster again.

But he is one of the lucky ones. Many children's families, especially in rural areas, have no resources such as telephones and transport to hospitals, and remain uninformed by medical authorities that more can be done to improve a patient's life. Jones attributes this to a "lack of pushiness" on the part of families, who think that rudimentary skin grafts, such as those performed on Sizwe Ndlovu, are "the best the doctor can do". What many do not know, she says, is that there are some state hospitals around the country that have highly specialised medical care and can "work wonders" with badly disfigured children.

They are few, though — all in urban areas, and with long waiting lists. This is off-putting to families who think that, with the worst of the physical damage healed, anything more is "cosmetic". But for children who have to leave hospital to face their family, schoolmates and peers, all the while knowing they look different, the trauma of being deformed is even worse than having dead skin scraped off in a hospital ward. Yet few hospitals offer post-burn counselling to the children and their families.

There are additional physical risks associated with being badly burned, such as increased susceptibility to skin cancer. Badly burned patients may also need physiotherapy, as skin tightening after burns affects the mobility of joints, especially in the arms and legs. This is not to mention the necessity of a high-protein, excellent diet to help the injuries heal quicker.

But when you are poor and you do not have the will or inclination to press big-time doctors in the city's academic hospitals to see your child, all these follow-ups are immense hurdles to be overcome. As one nurse at a paediatric burn unit says, shrugging her shoulders: "How can you tell someone who cannot even afford bread to buy tubs of aqueous cream?"

February 2 2001

NOTES & QUERIES

In old spy movies secret information was transmitted by a microdot, disguised as a full stop on a printed page. Did such things exist?

● Microdots still exist. It is an example of steganography, a system of communication that conceals not only the content of a message but the existence of the message itself. The technology was developed at the Dresden Institute by Emanuel Goldberg and others during the 1930s; from this German intelligence produced the microdot, which J Edgar Hoover called "the enemy's masterpiece of espionage". The process involved reducing a sheet of typewriter paper to the size of a postage stamp, then photographing the image through a reverse microscope, further reducing it. When developed and enlarged, it could reproduce an A4 typewritten page with perfect clarity. — *Professor William Dunlap, Quinnipiac University, Connecticut, United States*

● During World War II the FBI sent my father to Brazil to determine how Nazi sympathisers were able to send and receive information that enabled German U-boats to sink ships bringing supplies from the Americas to Britain.

My father developed a contact named "Tom", a Norwegian curio-store owner who had noticed that certain Germans regularly purchased breakfast trays decorated with the wings of butterflies glued to the base and covered with a sheet of glass. The Germans would buy a tray, take it away for a day or two, and then return, requesting that it be shipped to a German address. My father discovered that the butterfly wings had developed new markings under German hands — small black dots that turned out to be micro-formed information about the ships going out of North and South American harbours. Tom, whose father had been killed in the Nazi invasion of Norway, infiltrated German circles until he was able to determine the German in Brazil who was in charge. When informed of the plot, Brazil declared war on Germany. Tom went into hiding and my father was never able to trace him again — though he did name his first child Tom in his honour. — *Anita Hemphill McCormick, Los Angeles, US*

Tenants caught in crossfire after building 'hijacked'

Nawaal Deane

"Who should I pay?" most tenants are asking at the BG Alexander Building in Hillbrow, Johannesburg. Gladys Ndlovu stands outside the building with her tattered mattress up against a tree and the rest of her meagre belongings strewn around. On her back she carries her baby, wrapped in a threadbare blanket. "My husband is at the hospital. These people [collecting the rent] kicked us out and hit him," she says, wiping tears from her eyes.

Tenants are caught in the crossfire between two groups, the Africa Media University (AMU) and a group of "floor managers". Both claim "ownership" of the building. Each tenant pays R500 a month for a single room with no hot water. Approximately 1 000 tenants occupy the decrepit building, making it a lucrative business for whoever collects the rent.

Ndlovu's husband, Zenzo Khumalo, was taken to hospital on Tuesday for injuries he received when he refused to pay the rent. "The people collecting the rent do not own the building," says Khumalo, who comments that Edward Bruce, the former manager of AMU, brought in the floor managers who have now taken over the building. "If you don't want to pay they intimidate you and remove your stuff from the rooms. When I told them that they don't own the building they said I must not tell the other tenants and I must just pay what I can."

Khumalo refused. Fifteen gun-toting men attacked him and ordered him to "get out", he says. "They said, you are not paying us, why are you paying to the AMU account. They then pushed me against the wall and started throwing my things out."

The Department of Transport and Public Works owns the building, and leases it to AMU. In January last year, Liesl Göttert, AMU's CEO, signed a lease for a mere R100 a month in rental. The lease conditions specify that the premises cannot be sublet. Göttert denies any knowledge of the premises being sublet. In a statement to the police, she says Bruce — her former manager — hired people called "floor managers" to stop the illegal subletting. Bruce has now disappeared.

"I appointed Edward [Bruce] to oversee the academic side of AMU, and gave him the task to fill up the hostel blocks with live-in students," says Göttert. She said she visited the premises for the first time in December.

"On inspection it seemed apparent that the hostel blocks had been let out to people from the street and that the floor managers had been collecting deposits and rentals from tenants."

These floor managers claim that Bruce hired them on Göttert's instructions to fill up the hostels — not only with students, but with anyone willing to pay the rent. "We were the ones who had to clean this place and collect the rent and now they want to kick us out after they've realised how much money they can make," says Janet Wanjiru Nbugua, one of the floor managers.

The managers claim they had an agreement with Bruce: 50% of the rent would be deposited in AMU's bank account while the rest was theirs to keep. "We collected almost R50 000 for them in October," says Phumla Tau. "We clean this building and fix it," she says. The group brought in street children whom they employ to clean the building. However, Pastor Schedric Phiri, another tenant, says: "These are not street children but adult men who intimidate us to pay the rent."

Candice Golding, personal assistant to Göttert, claims the floor managers assaulted her when she tried to hand out memos stating that tenants should pay the rent into the AMU account. She has moved out of the building. "I feared for my life," she says. Gift Maseko, one of the floor managers, says: "Candice was living at the campus all the time but none of these tenants attended the community classes she was supposedly giving on Saturdays. How can these tenants be students?"

Each side accuses the other of theft and fraud. The tenants remain uncertain of their future. "I am too afraid not to pay the floor managers, but what will happen to us when they are gone?" asks Simon Ngubane, a 52-year-old tenant.

February 23 2001

Those teeth sink into the flesh of our humanity

David Beresford

There is a film in which Elliot Gould plays a photographer who makes a speciality of taking pictures of dog turds on the sidewalk. I cannot recall anything else about the film, not even its title, but that detail sticks in my mind.

I am reminded of it on such occasions as the World Press Photographic Awards, which seems to attach such a high premium to man's inhumanity to man. A great admirer of photographers, I faithfully attend that annual exhibition. But, rationalising that any attempt to take the sins of the world upon one's shoulders is to risk reduction to the manic and the messianic, I hurriedly move on from the news category and its decisive moments of horror. Besides, I reassure myself before pausing to glory in such as the decisive moment of a ballerina's leap, or a raindrop's fall, I have seen enough of atrocity for one lifetime.

It was in the suspicion that life tends to be composed of what one chooses to see — in the case of the Gould character, turds — that I found myself hurriedly switching off my TV last week when trying to discover whether George W Bush, aka "the Texan Poisoner", really had been chosen by the people of the United States to lead the world. The switch-offs were occasioned not by the disturbing sight of George Bush Mark II looking even blanker than his prototype, George Bush Mark I, but by the success South Africa had had in elbowing its way into world headlines just below those emanating from Florida.

After managing to survive much of the week without being exposed to the training techniques of the East Rand dog unit I received a call on Friday from my newspaper in London, expressing curiosity about the circumstances in which the upholders of law and order in this part of the world used human beings as dog meat. Dutifully I solicited a copy of the video from *Special Assignment* at the SABC and, after popping a capsule of St John's Wort in the vague hope it would prove a prophylactic against future nightmares, popped the cassette in the machine and, for the first time, watched.

I tried my best to convey in the article that I subsequently filed the full horror of 47 minutes in the day of a South African dog unit and the terror of 47 minutes ripped out of the lives of three black aliens who fell victim to it. There was the awful sense of the routine that attended the proceedings. There were the shouted orders: "Let the fucking dog go!"... "Look at the camera" ... "Kaffir, show where the dog bit you; nice, nice!" How the cameraman lingers over the bite wounds of the three with an almost lascivious attention. And the final act of savagery as two of the bulky policemen took turns in using the three battered and bleeding men as punchbags.

"That's a beauty," applauded one as a colleague sent a cowering black man sprawling with a straight right. "Let me have a go as well," he said, flattening the second with an uppercut and belting the third to his knees with a hook before finishing him off with two brutal kicks to the head.

But all the time I was writing, the inadequacy of verbal description was apparent to me. "A photograph is worth a thousand words," goes the old editorial rubric. And it was a striking aspect of the film that, although nobody died in the incident and far worse atrocities were reported in detail by the Truth and Reconciliation Commission, none of them had as much of an impact on the public consciousness as the antics of the dog unit.

Which invites an extension of the earlier rubric, with the observation that a few minutes of video convey more than an archbishop's five-volume accounting of "the truth", at least where South African security force atrocity is concerned. But why?

Flicking back through the memory banks I come up against an image that, in retrospect, probably traumatised me as a boy when I came across it in a public library. It was a photograph of a man in a concentration camp carrying a bucket that, the caption said, was full of human testicles. The shock effect of this picture was, when I think back to it, the familiarity of the bucket. The bucket was an ordinary bucket. I had carried just such a bucket on many occasions. I knew how a bucket's handle felt in my hand — the way it swung when it was empty and the way I staggered when it was full. I knew the uses of a bucket — in conjunction with a mop for cleaning the floors; my mother putting soiled underwear and socks in it with boiling water; builders carrying cement; my uncle on his farm carrying milk; myself tottering with a load of hot water determined to make up the mid-winter deficiencies of the bathroom geyser.

They were all part of the subconscious memories to which the brain resonates when confronted with the utilitarian, almost comforting image of a bucket. It is like the familiar chords of a song being played on a record that is torn apart by the caption ("human testicles"); the needle sent ripping through the vinyl tracks on the turntable to an accompanying shriek across the loudspeakers.

Fast-forwarding through memory I find myself peering again through the shattered walls of that church at Ntarama in Rwanda, at the assembled corpses of the prayerful dead. Again the mind resonates with familiar images — the pressure of praying knees on the floor, the warm and polished wood of the pews, the smell of the song book, the mellow chords of the organ, the cadences of the lesson, the fondly reproving look of a mother, the proud bass of a father, the mildly reproachful tones of the preacher — scattered by the shriek of the needle sent tearing into the mind by the smell and sight of rotting flesh slipping off skulls and skeletons.

And so it is with the dog unit. The blue fatigues of law and order, clothing the reassuring figures of authority. That shredded shirt there, it's like the one I bought at the flea market, amid the comforting hubbub of Saturday morning stalls!

The Alsatians; one guards my sleeping daughter at night, while another belonging to a cousin slobbers a wet tongue of welcome across my face, reducing me to splutters and my grandson to giggles.

Once again the needle rips as the familiar men in blue curse the familiar dogs on, sending their teeth tearing through the familiar shirts, into the familiar flesh of humanity, into friends and family, into my sleeping daughter, into my giggling grandson and into the collective memory until the shriek across the loudspeakers becomes just another track in our record of normality.

November 17 2000

Taxi satire gets the message across

Fred Esbend

A new form of public protest has hit the streets in Port Elizabeth — minibus taxi drivers are using their vehicles to broadcast their unhappiness with the government.

"Corruption ... Life's a bitch! Enjoy the ride" is emblazoned on the back of a taxi travelling through the city. Another taxi has a huge sticker that reads: "Ain't no gravy train ... We do the talk we do the walk."

A quick tour of the taxi ranks reveals more. On the back seat of a taxi the following is scribbled: "The Americans have Bill Clinton, Bob Hope, Johnny Cash and Stevie Wonder. We have Nelson Mandela, no hope, no cash, no wonder!" Another taxi highlights the government's failure to curb the crime rate: "Nationalise crime and make sure it doesn't pay". And: "Crime doesn't pay but the hours are good."

Former African National Congress war veteran Sipho Dlula says the use of satire on taxis is an ideal way of getting a message across to people and to remind them of "the ANC's failed election promises of a better life for all". Dlula is a taxi driver and hopes to own a taxi one day. He is disillusioned with the slow pace of economic transformation in South Africa, especially the government's failure to create jobs and its "inability to combat corruption within its own ranks".

Following convicted fraudster Allan Boesak's early release from prison, taxi driver Amos Kleinbooi pasted inside of his taxi a poem titled *A Prophet for Profit* that was written by an anonymous person under the pseudonym "Straight Talk". It reads: "There can be little doubt in anyone's mind/ Now Boesak's left his cell behind/ He'll take his title as Prophet-elect/ For profit which only he can collect/ With the ANC he'll walk the aisle/ To riches, luxury and style/ If it's prophecy you want, then this is mine/ The truth of which will come with time."

July 20 2001

Gauteng's newest citadel of sin

David Le Page

In Depression-era gangster films, amid clouds of smoke from tommy guns, the Feds occasionally managed to bust up great lorryloads of illicit liquor, sending whisky brewed and exported by the libertine Canadians pouring in torrents into the streets of Chicago.

Eighty years on, and a continent down and to the right, the penchant of law enforcement for licensed destruction is as robust as ever. Of late, TV news has regularly shown us illegal gambling machines heaped in scrapyard mounds before being pulverised by wrecking balls and trite conclusions.

Why have the authorities been doing this? The answer, dubbed Montecasino, rises in splendour from the pristine hills of Tuscany just north of Johannesburg, and opened a few weeks ago.

Over the past few years the nation has embraced legal gambling with the same fervour that it has poured into cellphones, offshore investment and kwaito. And the government has demonstrated unusual despatch in giving the industry its head. The destruction of illegal gambling machines assures the new venture and its kin their business, as neatly as apartheid-era laws assured Sol Kerzner his.

This monumental new casino/hotel/shopping mall complex has been painstakingly designed to look like a Tuscan village, coated with enough ochre to renew the walls of a thousand Parkhursts. The choice of a Tuscan aesthetic follows the same logic of spectacle that has seen pyramids rise in Las Vegas. Tsogo Sun's international partner in the Montecasino venture is United States gaming giant MGM Grand, and the concept architects for Fourways's new hill-top hamlet were US-based Creative Kingdom.

Tempting though it is, criticising Montecasino on grounds of taste would be absurd — and taste itself might resist being drawn into the argument. There is, though, one respect in which huge insensitivity has been demonstrated — the name chosen for this citadel of sin.

Monte Cassino was a 15-century-old Benedictine monastery, a great centre of European learning, before it was tragically destroyed by Allied bombing in one of the bloodiest battles of World War II. Many thousands of German, Polish and American soldiers died in its assault and defence. Parodying its name for the purposes of running a gambling joint is rather like naming a dental practice after Dachau or a pyrotechnics business after Dresden.

Montecasino's construction must have been a traumatic experience for the architects of record, Bentel Abramson & Partners, who appear to have been restrained from lovingly producing another horror along the lines of their earlier masterpiece, Sandton Square — Renaissance architecture with its eyes put out.

Entering the casino complex is rather like visiting a European necropolis during the height of the tourist season. Washing hangs from lines between the buildings, paralysed cocks leer from the roofs, ducks are poised in the middle of a stream, the old bicycle, motorcycle and battered Fiat are all there. But you know they will never again be used. The village appears lifelike, but the proper inhabitants are not there. They have fled before the invading army of tourists.

The village streets are lined with incredibly authentic metal and plastic bushes and trees, which also serve as convenient concealment for surveillance equipment. Namibian diamond enclaves are reputedly equipped for scanning the anuses of departing visitors and the removal of gem-trafficking pigeons from the skies with anti-aircraft fire.

Similar paranoia over security has led to the streets and alleys of Montecasino being completely roofed over. Then, in an effort to renew the illusion of an Italian village, the ceilings have been painted to resemble sky by day, by dusk and by night. But these painted firmaments induce a peculiar claustrophobia. One imagines it to be somewhat akin to the real condition called virtual reality sickness — nausea produced by a mismatch of sensory and motor feedback after being immersed in a computer-generated world. Here too, the normal focus of the eye is frustrated by imaginary distance. Emerge from the confines of the labyrinth, and as the real sky opens up above, the terror of infinite space proves warmly reassuring by contrast.

The designers do deserve tribute for their parking garage. It should serve as a lesson in low-budget ingenuity to all designers of industrial-scale office space, those who routinely inflict fluorescent lighting upon their victims. Over the parking bays, the light fittings have been painted yellow. The resulting illumination is far more comfortable than conventional fluorescent light.

Elsewhere, the same obsessive attention to detail has been paid to carving "stonework" from concrete walls and to creating "cobbled" paving just uneven enough to fool the feet into thinking they're tripping alongside authentic Italian peasantry. The outside of the complex, painstakingly painted to resemble battered plaster, almost appears to have suffered half a thousand years of weathering.

Yet in some of the interior domes, there seems to have been a rush to completion. Mouldings have been disdained in favour of crude *trompe-l'oeil*. Plans to put star-like lights in the night-sky roof were abandoned when it became clear such lighting would not be strong enough for the security cameras to work properly.

Still, in places the eye rolls comfortably down from a glowing, painted sunset, over stuccoed walls to convincing autumn leaves, before being disconcerted by the one-armed bandits crowding the village square. Montecasino is true to Italian reality in another respect — it is easy to lose one's bearings in the maze of streets, a problem no doubt welcomed by the retailers who line them. It makes one yearn for the familiar geometries of Sandton City or Hyde Park, not to mention the spiritual comforts of a simple shopping mall.

Ultimately, this mammoth construction demonstrates that, for the moment at least, South Africans seem to be far more adept at separating fellow citizens from their money than at helping each other become more prosperous. We have now a national lottery that takes money from those too poor to be squeezed in a casino, while the revenue service has become far more efficient than those arms of government charged with spending for the popular good. Equally, the lottery has yet to achieve the same success in disbursing its revenues that it has demonstrated in accumulating them.

Meanwhile, the crowds present at Montecasino even on a Sunday evening suggest it will be wildly successful. The complex is heir to the gaming rooms and enthusiasts who have for the past couple of years been resident at the Sundome, and it seems set to be even more popular. In Gauteng, financial expectations for the gambling industry are already being exceeded, even before all the region's planned casino developments have matured.

The enthusiasm of the public for surrendering its earnings to the taxman via submission to the most ruthless odds seems unbounded. Perhaps the government should embrace the logic of its skewed abilities: build a multitude of Montecasinos and abolish the revenue service. That at least would spread the satisfaction created by the industry to the many who choose not to gamble.

January 5 2001

What are you selling?

It is unbelievable that the *Mail & Guardian* would stoop to accepting the advertisement that has continued on page 7 over the past few weeks. I have continued to be repulsed and amazed at the vulgar display in the name of a product sale.

One finds it hard to miss the ubiquitous "full-metal woman", attired in a black lace-up bodice and adorned with a colourful garter belt, fully vented and ready to go, it would seem. Gleaming below is another woman's body, horizontal, supporting a powerful computer machine at or near the crotch area. If one looks to the extreme left of the horizontal figure, a nipple protrudes near the light that cascades off the body.

In what ways does this advertisement look to respect and value the role of women in South African society? Performing, supporting, being equated to a computer that one can turn on and off? — *Daniel E O'Leary, Cape Town; June 8 2001*

No pecs, no sex

Mercedes Sayagues

I have discovered the new erogenous zone for the new millennium. I am embarrassed it took me so long. But I may be excused: I hit the party circuit only a few months ago, when my last lover dumped me.

In more than one way, I was a casualty of the election in Zimbabwe. Those were electric, super-charged weeks. My neighbour, a bachelor in his late 20s, works for a South African oil company. Zim's fuel crisis stressed him, and everybody else. As did the forex crisis, the farms crisis, the violence crisis. I mean, the whole country was under stress. To decompress, my neighbour announced a party every Wednesday until the election, and a let-your-hair-down bash afterwards. If you can't beat them, join them. So I did, every Wednesday night, after filing my stories for the *Mail & Guardian*.

Rocky Horror Show was the first party's theme. The men were having a ball in fishnets and corsets, and spiked high heels were soon kicked off. The women looked like Morticia Addams or Dracula's friends, shrouded in black, baring little. I was definitively Ms Drab in my warm, woolly, writing clothes. The few men in civvies were soon shirtless. Mind, winter nights are cold in Harare. Maybe this is why women were wearing long sleeves. We were dancing to the hit: "You and me baby ain't nothing but mammals, so let's do it like they do on the Discovery Channel."

Suddenly I noticed that, at eye level, all I could see around me were male nipples. Male breasts wiggling like a Senegalese dancer shakes her hips or a stripper shows off her tits. All around, it was pecs, pecs and pecs. Men strutting their pecs.

What was I supposed to do about these hairless/hairy sweaty pecs at nose level? Lick the nipple? Pant with desire? Faint in immediate orgasm? I racked my head. I don't watch the Discovery Channel but I know what mammals do. What baffled me is what humans do. What does erotic etiquette prescribe these days?

Thus goes every party, albeit not in *Rocky Horror Show* garb. People arrive straight from work around 8pm. Dancing soon begins, men take off their shirts: pec parade is on. Women don't take their clothes off. They are voluntarily unsexy. The men are wild, oversexed, over the top.

Wiser now, I look around. Pecs are all over glossy mags, ads and fashion shoots. I ask around. "Pecs are sexy. It means a man takes care of himself," says a 28-year-old Aussie, Zimbabwe's lone tourist of the season. Over mochaccino, women describe last night's date as having "good pecs", not unlike men noting a "great bum". Mothers say their teenage boys spend hours bare-chested in front of a mirror.

"It's the gym culture," says an editor.

"No pecs, no sex" is the buzzword in American gyms. In a *New Yorker* cartoon, a thin, stylish woman tells a well-built guy: "Yes, let's do drinks if your breasts promise not to attack me." Vanity and body obsession have become trans-gendered. Will male pedicures be the next niche market? Male anorexia on radio talk shows?

And all this time I had not noticed pec-mania. I must have been very taken up with my last lover to miss this insight into the erotic *zeitgeist*. I thank the election for it and for a series of cool parties. The turmoil, however, cost me both my townhouse and my lover.

For the first, my landlord's farm was invaded and they needed the townhouse. For the second, this is what prompted our demise. I arrived home one day after interviewing torture survivors for five hours. On e-mail from Cape Town, lover boy waxed lyrical about "drumming up the late evening stars", flowing into heavenly ecstasies, and ended: "I hear bad news about Zimbabwe on the news. Is it flavour of the month among South African media or is some horrible calamity really happening there?"

I hit reply, and cut and pasted some quotes from my story-in-progress. Beginning with a man who had a bicycle spoke thrust into his anus and ,penis, and ending with, "Wake up to reality. It is uglier than you think."

That was the last I heard of him. He never replied. I didn't insist. I guess we both felt we live in different worlds. Here in Harare I am dealing with the likes of Dr Chenjerai Hitler Hunzvi while he is in Cape Town meditating with the likes of Guru Maharaj Ji. That relationship never had a future. Easy come, easy go.

But now that I think about it, he did have good pecs. Pity the parties were not on then, he would have been a hit.

September 29 2000

All that glitters, tingles and titillates

Suzanne Leclerc-Madlala

There is a joke making the rounds among pre-teen girls in KwaZulu-Natal that goes like this: "Why is Jennifer Lopez so poor? Answer: Because her love don't cost a thing." With reference to the title of this singer's hit song, the girls who giggle at this joke do so because they know (or should be starting to learn), that love should indeed cost a thing — many things in fact.

Older sisters share the schoolyard joke with younger girls at home, who laugh as well, but don't even know why. They are left to reflect on the meaning and inherent lesson. Aha, so love has a cost and the cost is measured in things.

When the time comes, they surely won't be so stupid, they won't be poor, their love will have its own proper price tag. They get the joke and the lesson is then registered somewhere in their mind, shaping their attitudes and expectations about love in today's South Africa.

Consumerist culture has cut a deep and wide swathe across all sectors of post-apartheid South African society. Along with places like China and Russia, South Africa's opening up to the world has entailed a mad rush towards, and eager pursuit of, all that glitters, tingles and titillates. Old struggle values no longer seem relevant in a society where materialism and consumerism define the new way forward. Activists and ordinary people alike have been sucked into the soft and spongy embrace of modernity's soulless money machine in the pursuit of pleasures that have little to do with nurturing a future. Given the magnitude of poverty, want and frustration that existed before 1994, perhaps this state of affairs was to be expected.

But in our present context of phenomenally high HIV/Aids rates, a growing reverence for "King Cash" might prove to be our undoing. HIV/Aids infection rates have skyrocketed and continue to do so despite all efforts of the past decade to halt the rapid spread of this disease. Researchers have tried to understand the nature of micro- and macro-dynamics that propel the virus, and to identify factors that could be manipulated to assist with behavioural change. We now know a fair deal about the social and behavioural "enablers" of HIV/Aids, and what we know is perhaps more depressing than not knowing anything at all. There are just so many dysfunctional component parts that play a role in shaping South African society as the world's foremost high-risk context for HIV/Aids.

What emerges most clearly is the fact that the type of social and economic changes needed to slow this epidemic will take a long time. During that time millions of people will be infected, millions will die, and in the process, new forces will emerge to drive the epidemic even faster and further afield.

One of these forces, as we are currently seeing, is associated with rising standards of living and increases in disposable income. It is not poverty itself that is a major factor in the growth of this disease in South Africa. Rather, it is poverty in the midst of wealth, or more appropriately, wealth in the midst of poverty. Perhaps even more appropriately, one way of understanding Aids in Africa more generally is as primarily a problem of men with money and women without.

There is currently a growing predation of young girls and women by older men. It's a trend that many say has started in the past few years and is one that will surely continue to grow. This will ensure that our high HIV/Aids rates remain with us for some time. This trend is tied directly to simultaneous increases in poverty among one (huge) sector of society and increases in wealth among another (small) sector of society.

For many, the 1990s have brought incredible opportunities for acquiring wealth, status and power where such things were formerly unobtainable. These new fruits of freedom have combined with old ways of thinking that have long equated power and status with increased access to women. A man's ability to attract and maintain a coterie of women has for eons been an index of manhood and a mainstay of patriarchal privilege in our sexist world.

In many societies today those notions still have wide currency. In modern-day South Africa, such measures of manhood are very much alive and well. In the context of astronomical HIV/Aids infection rates, the power-women-prestige complex is a great cause for concern. A man who cruises the country's urban ghettos in a shiny luxury car, accessorised with a cellphone on the dashboard and a chunky gold-ringed hand on the steering wheel, knows exactly what and who will look his way.

Research tells us that it is not only the material benefits that girls are after in their pursuit of sexual liaisons with these sugardaddies. Just the prestige derived from being seen in his expensive car is often enough, or the status that comes from being associated with Mr So-and-So. Research shows mothers often turn a blind eye to these liaisons. Keeping quiet while a daughter has her school fees paid, wears dresses that she herself cannot afford, and brings home groceries for the family is rapidly becoming a new form of silence for women in South Africa and another silence that nourishes Aids.

At the recent Aids conference at the University of the Witwatersrand, a group of young women presented their research findings on youth sexual dynamics in Alexandra township. Under a column marked "women's expectations" was listed "the three Cs". The women explained, in a lighthearted way, that this stood for the things women "needed" most (not "wanted" most). These things were cash, cars and cellphones. A participant asked why clothes were not included as one of the "Cs". One of the women responded that men cannot be trusted to make proper selections of clothing for women because they "don't know quality". For that reason the women preferred cash to buy their own.

In KwaZulu-Natal, young women speak jokingly of their "need" for several ministers in their lives; a minister of transport (he with the luxury car), a minister of finance (Mr Money Bags) and a minister without portfolio (a general good-time guy), or, as one woman remarked: "He could be the one that you actually liked or loved."

Such are the times in our fast-changing society that love and sex have come to have as much commodity value as most everything else. The lethal mixture of cheek-by-jowl poverty and wealth in South Africa with the growing incidence of both and a consumerist "get it while you can" social ethos will ensure that we will remain world leaders in HIV/Aids rates for some time. The social performance of male sexual power and privilege will continue to be enacted in ways that drive the epidemic, and the obvious need for jobs, water and roofs over heads will continue to justify scoffing at calls for greater gender equity.

Perhaps it is time to give up cracking our heads over why behavioural change has not occurred amid relatively high levels of HIV/Aids awareness. Maybe we underestimated the power and misinterpreted the nature of the combined forces that swept into life in the new South Africa. Maybe we just did not know what kinds of strengths would be needed to manage the transition process. Maybe we still don't know, and maybe we won't really care. Maybe it should be just as it seems — time to let the good times roll and leave the future to look after itself.

June 15 2001

Merc mania

Krisjan Lemmer

Oom Krisjan is glad to see his old friend Chief Mangosuthu Buthelezi taking such a strong line on corruption and the culture of entitlement. The chief — who must have missed a *Mail & Guardian* article last week exposing his R750 000 housing freebie funded by the taxpayer — told the Inkatha Freedom Party national conference in Ulundi at the weekend: "We did not engage the difficult road to transformation just to see a handful of people living in grand houses and entertaining fancy habits."

Warming to the subject and referring to what Oom Krisjan can only assume to be the Yengeni Mercs, the Inkatha leader continued: "The struggle was not waged for a few people to get smart cars."

At that point Inkatha's sole serving provincial Premier, Lionel Mtshali, awoke from his slumber. Having caught the tail end of his chief's speech, he decided not to be outdone. Reporting to the party faithful on his post as premier, Mtshali boasted that the "highlight" of his year was the procurement of a R1,8-million armoured Mercedes Benz S500 limo for Zulu King Goodwill Zwelethini and another five cars for the king's wives.

Turning to housing, Mtshali recounted as another highlight of his premiership the establishment of a "department of the royal household" with a dedicated budget of almost R21-million, up R4,3-million from the previous year. Sorry, Gatsha, but Oom Krisjan thinks Mtshali gotcha.

July 13 2001

What is the source and origin of the word *fundi*? I have spoken to friends in Europe, United States, Australia and New Zealand and no one has any idea. It therefore seems to have a South African root.

● This is Bantu in origin. In the Swahili language *fundi* means expert. Repairers of watches, cars, electronics and so on, are usually called *fundi* due to their expertise in their work. *Fundisha* means to teach, so it is only a *fundi* who can expertly transfer knowledge about his/her expertise. It therefore has a Swahili root, as do safari and panga, words that have found their way into English. — *Chrispo Caleb Okumu, Johannesburg*

● The word *fundi* is derived from Zulu (and other Bantu languages) where the verb *funda* means read, learn or study, and the noun *umfundi* means a learner, a student, a scholar or an expert. It is in the last sense that it is used as the South African equivalent of the United States *guru*, or the British *boffin,* both of which are also used in South Africa, but I think the indigenous term is better. In East Africa it has a more manual connotation. In Swahili *fundi wa saa* is a watch repairer, and not someone designing a time travel machine. — *Steve Hayes*

● About 30-million South Africans know the answer. It is derived from the Xhosa word *imfundi*, meaning an expert. (Not to be confused with *umfundisi* meaning teacher.) — *Ferdie Klian, Uitenhage*

A queen for a night

Marianne Merten

What is one to think when an eight-year-old girl appears on stage during a beauty pageant dressed in see-through lace and a black G-string? Are her ambitions the same as those of the young women of the Miss World or Miss South Africa competitions who no doubt will always profess to want to save the world with their flashing smiles and tresses? Or is it a case of girls being told from an early age that their bodies, smiles and sexuality can secure a better future?

It is Saturday night and about 50 hopefuls, aged from six to their late teens, take to strutting their stuff in the Miss Manenberg competition. The girls are preened — hair teased and sprayed into sculptured beehives or tumbling curls — beautified by make-up and dressed to the nines. Steps are rehearsed: across the stage, along the front, a stop and a bit of eye contact and a large smile before the judges. Hips are swaying, heads held high.

Manenberg is one of the toughest neighbourhoods on the Cape Flats. Gangsters dominate the poverty-stricken area where unemployment is estimated at more than 70%. Teenage pregnancy is common, as is jack-rolling: the abduction and rape of young women and girls either as part of a gang-initiation ritual or as revenge because a male relative failed to perform a favour for a gang or join a gang.

But for one night these girls are queens. Their proud mothers sit in old tracksuits or jeans and T-shirts with their hair under doekies or in curlers in the audience, shouting encouragement and ordering their offspring to smile, smile, smile. Old shoes are reinvigorated with sequins for the formal-wear appearance. Clearly, many of the younger girls wear new jeans and funky T-shirts for the casual section. Evening dresses have been crafted from pieces of sequinned material or from an elder sister's dress.

White lace is the definite favourite in the evening section among the very young. Figure-revealing Jennifer Lopez-type dresses or a skimpy top and full-length skirt combo held together with chains in all the right places dominate the evening wear for the older girls. Some of them have already revealed most in the casual section with hot pants and boob tubes à la American gangster rap music video extras.

I am one of the judges — called in at the last minute. My fellow arbiters of beauty are a woman priest and a photographer. We take our duties seriously, conscious of the prying eyes of any mother particularly keen that her daughter should win. After all, we joked earlier, there may be trouble from the audience if we make the wrong choices. Rumour is that this happened before.

There is to be a Miss Personality, two princesses and a queen for each of the four age categories: four to six, seven to nine, 10 to 12, and older. Walk, dress and personality (read smile) are the three marks on the basis of which the girls are ranked.

I'm not sure how the other judges arrive at their scores. But the girl who has the guts to walk on stage in a plain denim dress as formal wear and still smile — her fellow competitors wore satin, lace and sequins with the occasional set of matching gloves — got one of the highest scores for personality from me. And I have to admit I find it disturbing, and accordingly deduct points, when an eight-year-old shakes her (non-existent) breasts underneath a skimpy lace dress.

In spite of the obvious pains someone has taken to pile loops and loops of hair into a daring triangular creation, it looks out of place on a nine-year-old.

What becomes clear that night is that the girls already know their smiles, their bodies and the way they use it will bring results: peer approval, social standing or maybe a better boyfriend.

As the evening progresses the music becomes louder and louder. Later we find out the DJ and his friends are having a private party with a few quarts in the sound box upstairs regardless of the twirls below. The audience does not mind the pageant turning into a disco either: it is Saturday night and there are few safe places to go to in Manenberg.

After 10pm the young men arrive. When the 12 and older age group takes to the stage, cat calls and whistles are heard over the music as the guys check out the girls. Younger siblings, tired of sitting on hard plastic chairs, move towards the stage to dance to the music and shout encouragement to their favourites.

As the evening ends past midnight and everyone files out of the community hall, one mother turns around and says: "Good choices!" And I find myself hoping that at least some of the girls will take the confidence they showed on stage beyond the evening's glamour.

December 15 2000

'You're too young for sex'

Suzan Chala

The rights to confidentiality and privacy, informed consent and access to health care are in South Africa's "patients' rights charter". But at Pimville clinic in Soweto, these seem to be privileges rather than rights. Teenagers seeking advice and treatment on sex, pregnancy and sexually transmitted diseases (STDs) are sent from pillar to post in a bureaucratic maze, refused treatment and sometimes insulted by medical practitioners at the clinic.

Palesa Tlou (17) and Thato Lebese (18), both high school students, were refused pregnancy testing at the clinic. One nurse told Tlou she was "too young to get involved in sexual activities. What do you know about pregnancy?" Another told Lebese that she couldn't get a pregnancy test just because she was "late".

Dressed in a school uniform, posing as a 17-year-old, I visited the Pimville clinic. Patients stand in a queue from 6.30am. When the clinic opens at 7am they are treated to a church service performed by a nurse. I'm still in a queue after what seems like a lifetime of waiting when the administrator shouts: "Those who are here for pregnancy tests should go to the ANC." What does a political party have to do with pregnancy tests? Finally a cleaner explains that the ANC is the antenatal clinic.

At the desk where you queue for a card you are required to explain why you have come to the clinic. Trying not to be heard by other patients I whispered: "I have come for a pregnancy test, HIV test and STD test." The nurse, obviously irritated, ordered me to speak louder. When I did so she shouted at me, telling me that I was "a pain in the neck", that I "want too many things" and that the clinic does not have pregnancy test kits.

A sympathetic nurse called me to a corner and showed me to a room where I "would get help". I peeped at the other patients' cards in a queue: written on all of them was "STD". In the consultation room, the nurse locked the door and asked me to explain what the problem was. "You people are told every day about HIV/Aids, but you still don't use condoms and when you get it you start blaming people saying that they treat you badly," she shouted.

After the examination she gave me pills and when I asked what was wrong with me she said "an STD". "Which one?" I asked. "Please leave," was her answer. She told me I did not meet the requirements for an HIV test, which is to contract an STD. But she had just told me that I had an

STD, despite the fact that a recent examination I had at a private hospital proved that I was healthy and STD-free.

The Gauteng Department of Health condemned the actions of health practitioners at these clinics, saying they were a "violation of the patient's rights' charter".

August 3 2001

Incest is family custom, says dad

James Hall

Generations of fathers in Jasper Nxumalo's family of Hhohho, Swazi-land, have found an expedient and, they say, biblically sanctioned way to achieve primogeniture, or obtain a male heir: incest with a daughter.

"I slept with my first-born daughter because it is family custom to do so," Nxumalo told the Mbabane Court of Appeal this week while seeking to have his conviction overturned for rape and incest. "My father did the same, my grandfather did it, and my great grandfather did it, too."

A trio of appeal court judges sat alternately stonefaced and slack-jawed as Nxumalo explained that the rape of the eldest daughter is required to secure a male heir to the family homestead. "This is even in the Bible," he told the court, citing chapter and verse from Genesis and I Corinthians 7:36: "If she pass the flower of her age, and need so require, let him do what he will, he sinneth not."

The Nxumalo family values did succeed in producing an heir. After being forced to have sex with her father for four years, beginning in 1992 when she was nine years old, Nxumalo's daughter fell pregnant in 1996, when she was 13, and gave birth to a boy the following year.

Public prosecutor Musa Nsibandze was not permitted to rise from his chair and present the crown's case. Judge Herbert Shearer told him not to bother as he had heard enough from the defendant to uphold Chief Justice Stanley Sapire's original conviction. Shearer only regretted the brevity of Nxumalo's nine-year jail term. Nxumalo left the court complaining bitterly that his family custom would never have come to light if his estranged wife, now remarried, had not urged his daughter to reveal to police the identity of her child's father.

His former wife has been seeking therapy for the girl from councillors attached to the Swaziland Action Group Against Abuse. The Manzini-based anti-abuse NGO is pleased with the conviction. Incest cases are increasing, but court sentences have been rare. Councillors urge abuse victims to report their tormentors to the police. Police in turn bring rape victims to the group's councillors for assistance.

Is incest to achieve primogeniture an honoured Swazi custom in rural areas? At least two previous defendants claimed the same thing when they were tried for incest. Khosi Mthethwa, director of the anti-abuse group, is incredulous about this "custom". "The current case is clearly a copy-cat of previous attempts to use this defence," she says. "When we first heard about this 'custom' we did extensive research, including focus groups with traditionalists and elders. We found no evidence that incest was ever tolerated in Swazi society."

A theologian, Jabulani Dlamini, scoffs at the notion that biblical passages given by defendants are justification for incest. "The selection of verses mentioned in court was nonsensical. The ones cited from Genesis were merely 'so-and-so begat so-and-so', and the Corinthians passage was taken out of context." Dlamini doubts any church in Swaziland advocates incest.

But church sanctioning is apparently unnecessary for some men in the kingdom. Mthethwa's statistics show reported cases of abuse are up 50% on last year. Abuse cases fall into three categories: physical, including rape and incest; emotional, such as threats and bullying; and economic, where a husband takes all his wife's earnings, sometimes leaving the family to starve, because by Swazi law a woman is a legal minor.

"Part of the increase is due to better reporting, but some of it is an actual rise in abuse crimes," she says. "In the southern Shiselweni district, there has been an influx of unemployed miners who were retrenched from mines in South Africa, and some are taking out their misfortune on spouses and children." But some cases are appearing in court, with convictions taking place despite claims of customary privilege.

December 8 2000

The costs of living with Aids

Dianne Black

Richard, a part-time employee of very long standing, had been steadily losing weight and suffering from recurrent bouts of illness. When he told me that he had had swollen glands for weeks and they would not go down despite the medication he had been receiving, I didn't have to be a physician to suspect what might be wrong.

My general practitioner (GP) was discretion itself. Richard (not his real name) would need to have some blood tests. No, he did not know what was wrong. No, he could not suggest what it might be. Only once the initial tests were done and Richard had given his permission were my husband and I brought into the discussion.

And that is when theory gave way to experience and we began really to understand that for the millions who are not Richard, who do not have access to caring private doctors, easy transport, convenient clinics, information and, above all, relatively large bank accounts — their own or those of somebody willing to help — HIV-positive may indeed be a death sentence.

It is only once we found ourselves in a sense "living with Aids" that we realised how very little the average privileged South African knows about how to deal with it. What were we in for? What could we do? Where could we find the information we needed to help a man who has been in our lives for more than 25 years handle something he clearly did not understand? We were on a learning curve.

So was Richard. The first thing he had to do, counselled the GP, was to go home and tell his wife and family. How? The GP gave me the number of a hospice that, in turn, put me on to the dedicated counsellors in a clinic in Esselen Street, Johannesburg. Had Richard not already had the blood tests done, they would have organised those for him.

But where to go for the triple drug cocktail that would control the rampant virus that had invaded his bloodstream? Perhaps we were particularly ignorant. Perhaps, influenced by the reams that have been written about abandoned Aids clinics in hospitals, we didn't even try what might have turned out to be an easily accessible option. Our GP knew little more than we did. He knows he will ultimately have to learn a whole lot more but the problem is only now beginning to filter into his northern suburbs practice.

Here too, though, we are fortunate in our ability to access a range of contacts.

Through a close friend who works actively in the fields of Aids activism and is, himself, HIV-positive, we were referred to a private medical practice specialising in the problem. Here Richard was examined; counselled; told simply, quietly and insistently what drugs were being prescribed and exactly how he should take them; and assured that if he encountered problems, advice was at the end of a telephone line.

He doesn't discuss it. We don't ask. He has his drugs. We hope he will take them and live to enjoy a relatively healthy and economically active life for many years. We don't know what we will do if he becomes really ill. We are concerned and not a little frightened by the prospect of lingering, terminal illness. But if the time comes we will find a way to handle that too. We have the resources and the access to information.

If Richard did not have anyone to fall back on how would he cope? The answer has to be that he, like millions of South Africans, would not cope at all; he would simply get sicker and sicker, be unable to work to support himself or his family, and eventually die, probably in abject poverty.

The costs we have run up so far look like this: Private doctors, several consultations — around R500; blood tests, private laboratory — around R1 000 (a second set will be done in six weeks at much the same cost to determine whether the medication is working); drugs — R978 a month, if the pharmacy does not offer them at cost, R685 if it does.

Had this problem arisen four years ago, those drugs would probably have totalled in excess of R4 000 a month. We are assured that at some time in the future the cost will decrease even further. Perhaps it will. Perhaps it won't. We can't wait. Perhaps the government will stop ducking and diving and take steps to make the drugs available to those who need them most and can afford them least. Perhaps they won't. Those people can't wait either.

For the price of a multibillion-rand defence contract, a presidential jet, a clutch of official Mercs, millions of South Africans could remain economically active, could have a future, could be given a chance. But they won't. A country has to have its priorities. Doesn't it?

Poverty, it has been said, contributes to the spread of Aids. There may be some truth in that. What is certain, though, is that Aids contributes to the spread of poverty.

August 3 2001

Anything goes ...

Themba ka Mathe

What can a writer say about a poet he failed to write about eight months ago, when the poet's maiden book hit the South African market? Nothing. Poets are boring people. Aren't they? Usually, unless the poet is Kgafela oa Magogodi.

I find myself at the Wits University sports grounds on a recent Sunday afternoon. Tension is thick in the air until two soccer teams eventually settle for a draw. Five minutes earlier a thickset striker glided past two defenders only to miss a scoring opportunity. It's unartistic, especially when the striker is Oa Magogodi. "Anything goes," he tells me.

Indeed, anything goes for this poet masquerading as a footballer. First he took his poetry to the stage, then into knock-and-drop pamphlets, later into a book and now he is taking it to the big screen. The big question as he leaves for New York for a six-week film-making course is whether the literary world is losing him. "It's difficult to decide what the governing principle of your spirit is. But I'm always open to change and growth, because one always encounters experiences that changes him."

Oa Magogodi has experienced many twists of fate in his 33 years of multiple roles as a son, father, husband, musician, poet, filmmaker, Wits PhD student and lecturer. One twist was at Fuba, the institute of music Oa Magogodi joined in 1988. At the time, he says, he just wanted to sing. Sipho Sepamla was a director and Don Mattera ran the art gallery. Then followed a stroke of luck that was to propel Oa Magogodi into a career as a poet.

When Mattera came to talk to his class, Oa Magogodi was asked to deliver the vote of thanks. "Throughout his recital I formulated my speech. When I went up front I masqueraded as a poet." Mattera believed him and with every poem Oa Magogodi subsequently wrote and sent to Mattera for criticism, he also started to believe in himself. Mattera has been his spiritual father ever since.

"He had an instant impact and we still maintain the connection. I go to him if I want to speak to an elder." Oa Magogodi has impressed his mentor and has earned his respect. "He has reached a certain plane of social consciousness. If many of our youth do the same, we will move faster," says Mattera. "It's rare for young people to speak their minds and feelings, they normally express that through their actions." Oa Magogodi penned *Congas for Zinga,* a tribute to Mattera that is included in his book *Thy Condom Come.*

The younger poet still has colourful memories of Fuba's yearly Steve Biko commemorations, when a group of singers couldn't make sense of his doodling lyrics. For the benefit of the singers, his lecturer ordered him to read it with the band playing in the background. Instead of reading, he rapped. And Oa Magogodi's journey as a performance poet started.

In 1993, while reciting poetry at Kippie's, he encountered a swearing poet by the name of Lesego Rampologeng. "I used to be shy because I thought I was swearing. When I saw this guy doing the rap attack, I got inspired to write and recite freely."

A batch of things and people has shaped this poet. His poetry has echoes of Dambudzo Marechera, Mattera, Rampologeng and Sepamla. "Look, not one single writer is created in a vacuum. I have created my voice from all the voices that I have listened to," he says. "I rhyme when I want to ... But playing with a band can be very restrictive. It's almost like jazz skating, finding one's voice in the sound."

He is no ordinary musician. In his performance the pure word prevails, despite the power of the sound, and there is a certain musicality about the natural rhyming of his word. If you did not see him perform in Holland early this year, I don't blame you — the venue was sold out when he rocked the Linton Kwesi Johnson stage. Kick yourself if you missed his linguistic chisel at the Grahamstown arts festival. Shame on you if he has not yet shattered your ears in clubs and pubs around Johannesburg or at the Windybrow Theatre recently.

Wits lecturer Phaswane Mpe says listening to Oa Magogodi's poetry and songs is a shattering experience. "I guess I was shocked by his vulgarity ... Each line throws a defiant question at you and ... forces you to search deeper into the cultural-political dynamics of South Africa, as well as the complexities of the country's individual souls."

But what is Oa Magogodi's work about? Social commentary? Partly. Political commentary? Partly. A list of complaints? No. It may be an utter misreading, even an affront, to discern specific suggestions, given that all things seem allowable in experiment. With Oa Magogodi anything goes. His poetry skates, consciously or otherwise, between rap, beat, hip-hop and shit. But he has made it his mission to be the one reflecting the prevailing situation. Whether it's Aids, feminism, homosexuality, crime or life in general, he tries to be there.

Oa Magogodi's oeuvre also indicates an affirmation, confrontation and celebration of his personal background, environment, family and world culture, referring constantly to the memory of his upbringing by a poetic grandfather. "Our identities are far from being clear. People should decide what they want me to be. You cannot police people's perceptions about who they think you are.

"Look, I write because I'm located in a community that is in need of my talent. I don't want to police boundaries because we have gone beyond that stage where people must write about this and not about that. My writing is a celebration of life, whom I sleep with and whom I don't sleep with."

I look at Oa Magogodi and think, "Here is a promising black scholar and public intellectual in the making." But even with a future looking so bright, it has not been smooth sailing for this Soweto-born, Mafikeng-bred boy. He left Fuba in 1989 because of financial troubles. In the next few years he "chaired the African Writers' Association [the Sol Plaatje branch] in Mafikeng and encountered a lot of Pan-Africanist writers. The spirit of struggle and resistance was awakened in me."

But there was pressure from home. The commands came from daddy and were clear. "You either look for a job, son, or go back to school." He chose school. In 1993 he did a bridging course at Khanya College for a degree programme at Wits University. When he completed his degree he was invited to design a course on African cinema, oral performance and rap/dub poetry studies. Oa Magogodi had entered Wits through the side door, survived and excelled where many a black student feels alienated. "I did not go there to train for a job. For me, it was a matter of understanding myself. I knew what I wanted, because I was already a poet and musician then, so my terrain was defined already."

On the way to getting his work in print he endured, he says, much spiritual pain. The more he wrote poems the more another idea plagued him. "Publishing for me meant that my work would spread and even be accessible when I was not performing," he says. This was to be the beginning of a journey of excuses and unfulfilled promises. The responses from publishing houses ranged from the standard "poetry does not sell" to the encouraging "we are not publishing poetry at the moment" to the dispiriting "you are swearing".

"I decided to do it my own way." His free pamphlets went as far as the University of Natal, where a lecturer bought one of them for R5. When he got a call from the lecturer asking for permission to use it in his classes, the aspirant poet was saddened and thrilled. "Those pamphlets were not meant to be sold, but at the same time I was excited that someone was already using my work to lecture."

Then last year, while on a European tour with his band, he played to full houses in France and Germany and realised how important his work was to people. He eventually met his publisher in Holland. "We were hoping for a recording deal, but I eventually got a publishing one. At first I thought it was one of those things, because I had been promised it in this country before." It took three months of communication (editing, re-editing and cover designing) by e-mail to get *Thy Condom Come* out. "I felt great to have my material in a book format. I'm not even worried about what people say about the material in there. My work as an artist is to produce."

His introductory poem, *ke Magogodi*, is in Setswana, which many would say is short-changing non-Setswana readers, but he vehemently disagrees. "Literacy is not about English alone. So people must learn." And now that he has broken into publishing he is confident that next year his experimental stories and more poems will be out.

"I have got a problem with this notion that young black people don't write," he says. "Writing does not only exist in book form. That's literary deafness. You should come and see young poets and writers expressing themselves at reading sessions."

July 27 2001

NOTES & QUERIES

Do women have a masculine side that they might find advantageous to get in touch with?

● Obviously women have a masculine side and it should also be obvious to anyone that the things we consider feminine or masculine are actually complementary attributes that should be developed in every individual. We also still don't really know what comes from genetics/ nature and what comes from upbringing or the environment. — *Ian Barrett, Cape Town*

● If one insists on thinking in terms of gender stereotypes, it should be noted that women who participate in the labour force have, by definition, had to get in touch with their "masculine" side. To be successful in unpaid reproductive work women are required to acquire skills in time management and dispute mediation, as well as to endure exhausting physical labour and be on call 24-hours a day. I find it hard to imagine what more women might wish to do to emulate stereotypically male behaviour. Plunder, pillage and rape? — *Blackwell, St Catharines, Ontario, Canada*

Brown condoms for clever dicks

Belinda Beresford

I t's all in the packaging! That, at least, is the hope of the Department of Health, which has decided that colour counts in the battle against Aids.

In an attempt to make condoms more popular among the majority population, government-sponsored Condom Cans could soon be stocked with brown condoms as well as the white ones. Nono Simelela of the Aids directorate in the Department of Health says research has found some black men find white condoms off-putting.

For reasons of cost the Department of Health's foray into more exotic intimate action wear is likely to be limited to extending the colour range for the time being.

But condom manufacturers worldwide are doing their best to make safer sex fun. Condoms have been around since the pharaohs, made from fish bladders and animal gut before the advent of latex and polyurethane. No one knows where the name condom comes from, but one likely suggestion is that it derives from the Latin word *condus* or receptacle. People who pull a condom over their head as a party trick, fill them with water to use as water bombs, or blow them up as impromptu balloons, will tell you that there is no such thing as a small condom. True, they stretch. The problem for some men is that if the fit is tight around more sensitive areas, it dulls the nerves and reduces pleasure. And gaining pleasure is, after all, the reason why men are wearing them.

Men come in different shapes and sizes. Consider the issue of girth: research suggests that about 42% of men have a penis that is widest at the head; in 27% of cases it is widest on the shaft, and in 12% at the base. Which is why condoms come with different shapes as well as widths and lengths to accommodate the cornucopia of man. If your local pharmacy doesn't have an enticing enough range, take a trip to the many retailers on the Internet such as Condomania (www.condomania.com) where "Clever Dick" will help you chose your ideal wrapper from a wide range of choices.

Some men find it's more enjoyable having a condom that is looser around the head of the penis where there are many nerve endings. Condom manufacturers have risen to the challenge, creating ergonomically designed condoms with built-in "wriggle room" such as the Pleasure Plus and the inSpiral. It's not just size that matters; warmth plays a role. The problem is the thicker the condom the less easily men feel the warmth of their partner's vagina or anus. Durex has reported that the difference in temperature between the man's penis and the vagina can be up to 4°C. This is one of the advantages of the polyurethane condom — very thin and a good heat conductor — widely regarded as the Z3 of condoms.

For the real extrovert, you can buy a musical condom. But the most intriguing condom the *Mail & Guardian* has encountered was a glow-in-the-dark number. Not that unusual: sex educators have said men like them "so they can see where they are going" — or, one presumes, coming. But the wrapper of this one contained a lengthy disclaimer that it was not a preventative against pregnancy, HIV or sexually transmitted diseases, and warned that it should not be worn during any form of penetration. Which raises the image of a glowing love club being waved enticingly in a darkened bedroom as part of a human mating dance.

September 21 2000

NOTES & QUERIES

Is it wrong to be wealthy?
● When a friend of mine helped me out of a financial hole he stifled my embarrassed protests by outlining his philosophy. "Money," he said, "is like horse manure. If you spread it around, it can do a lot of good. If you just leave it where it is, all you've got is a pile of shit." I'd often wondered what the smell was in certain large houses. — *Adam Forde, Haslemere, Surrey*
● If you came across a child drowning in a pond, then it would be indefensible not to act. Similarly, it is indefensible to be inactive in the face of Third World poverty and famine. That those dying are thousands of miles away, and that there are mil-

lions of other people who can also help but remain inactive, is insignificant. The only justifiable course of action is to give away your wealth to help these people, until the marginal loss for yourself is equivalent to the marginal gain of the recipient. — *John Hampson, Chester*
● Only if it's right to be poor.— *Paul Wiseman, Rio de Janeiro, Brazil*
● The most thorough, perceptive, enlightening and entertaining answer to this question that I know of is Bernard Shaw's sadly neglected masterpiece *The Intelligent Woman's Guide to Socialism, Capitalism, Sovietism and Fascism.* — *John Broderick, South Africa*

Pricks on the inside

Krisjan Lemmer

L emmer cannot help but giggle with amusement and respect when Evita Bezuidenhout, aka Pieter-Dirk Uys, arrives in town on her determined campaign to beat the HIV/Aids plague with educated laughter. This week Evita was back in Parliament entertaining staff and MPs equipped with two large rubber penises, one black and one white.

"You have to be terribly clear about exactly what is going on," Evita explained, pretending to be a sex educator giving a condom demonstration to schoolchildren using a plastic banana. "This is a banana, this is a penis. The condom goes on the penis, not on the banana ... I don't think anyone's ever hauled out a condom in this chamber," she added to roars of laughter.

It was three years ago that Evita breached the walls of parliamentary prudery to put on a hilarious performance in the old assembly chamber. On that occasion she used a large, phallic cactus — explaining she liked it, because unlike party caucuses "the pricks are on the outside".

Lemmer would like to have extended his admiration to Parliament for the sense of enlightenment it shows in hosting these sexually explicit performances. Unfortunately its record in that respect was besmirched this time around by a ban on photographers and television cameras. Seems there are still pricks on the inside.

March 30 2001

Faulty logic and false theology

Cosmas Desmond

A ccording to the Catholic bishops, the morals of our country are being undermined by "lack of self-control and lack of respect for others ... unfaithfulness and irresponsible sexual behaviour ... loose living". In other words, "morality" equals sexual morality — a decidedly pre-Vatican Council II view of Christian ethics and of the church.

The Roman Catholic Church is the one true church; the rest are heretics or schismatics who have strayed from the one true path of Rome. And sex is something essentially dirty, which can be only tolerated for the purpose of propagating the human race. Why bother?

I would have thought that the selfish pursuit of wealth, consumerism, greed, and lack of concern for the poor were far more responsible for the decline of morals (when were they inclined?) in our country. After all, according to the Bible, depriving the labourer of his hire is a sin crying out to heaven for vengeance. It does not say that about wearing a condom.

Further, "lack of self-control" does not only apply to sex. What about drink — for which Roman Catholic clergy are renowned — anger, etc? When I was a missionary priest, I found that the worst criticism the people could make of a priest was *"unolaka"*: he was angry and short-tempered and shouted at people.

They were not concerned about his sex life. And they never told me who was the father of the coloured boy who bore a striking resemblance to one of my predecessors.

Apart from any other considerations, of which there are many — such as the sexual history of some of those who were party to the statement — it is exceedingly arrogant of the Catholic bishops, and an insult to other church leaders, to claim that they are the only ones who are concerned with morality. Many Anglican, Methodist and oßther church leaders, who are at least as dedicated Christians as their Roman counterparts, support the use of condoms, but they are not advocating sexual promiscuity. Are they responsible for destroying the moral fibre of our country? Are the Catholic bishops the only upholders of Christian morality? Why is it that those who — officially — do not have sex are so obsessed with it? Sex may be the source of life, but there is also more to life.

Further, if they are to pontificate — berobed in their transvestite glory — about morality, they should stick to morals and not indulge in pseudo-scientific argument — as our president does. What evidence, for example, does Cardinal Wilfred "abortion is the cause of all evil" Napier have for saying that condoms may be one of the main causes for the spread of Aids? Does he really think that people say, "Hey, here's a condom, let's have sex"? Rather, they say, "Let's have sex — condom or not." Get real, Cardinal. If that is possible for a Roman-trained Canon lawyer.

In my experience, as one who — defying all human logic — remains an adherent of the Roman Catholic Church, I have found that those clergy of other denominations who are happy with their sexuality are far more concerned about the real issues, such as justice and concern for the poor. Pope Pius XII, unlike many popes, was doubtless virginal until his death: how did that help the Jewish victims of the Nazis? Does it matter whether the priests and nuns who were party to the genocide in Rwanda were celibate or not? Did the crusaders only pillage and not rape? Does the chastity of the clergy who defended apartheid exonerate them?

The Catholic Church has been preaching and teaching for something like 2 000 years that sex is nasty and dirty and that if you indulge in it outside marriage you will be eternally condemned to the fiery torments of hell. Yet it still remains a very popular pastime — even among the clergy. If such a threat does not deter people, why should the threat of Aids? People, especially young people, are going to continue to have sex, whatever the church or anybody else says. Even if, because they use a condom, they do not create new life, at least they will reduce the risk of ending one.

Even in terms of orthodox Roman Catholic moral theology, it can be argued that using a condom to prevent transmitting Aids, rather than to prevent conception, is justifiable. The bishops partially acknowledge this in relation to married couples. But their logic is as faulty as their theology. If, as they claim, they are "pro-life" — despite the church having waged wars and supported the death penalty for centuries — why are they not concerned about the tens of thousands of babies who are being condemned to a painful and premature death each year because of the government's refusal to treat pregnant women and their babies with nevirapine? Without the use of condoms, there will be even more of them. Viva death!

August 10 2001

Ludicrous and unscientific

The South African Catholics bishops' stance against the use of condoms to curb the spread of HIV is irresponsible. Not only is the debate 15 years too late, it is totally out of touch with the suffering of so many people.

The assertion that "condoms may even be one of the main reasons for the spread of HIV/Aids" is ludicrous and unscientific. The bishops sound like the Saducees of old and certainly not like the life-affirming healer Jesus. Surely the bishops ought to walk the talk of life and compassion? It is shameful that they have not offered pastoral guidance during this time of confusion and despair.

Our only hope is that religion is no longer the opium of the people and that good sense will prevail. — *Mark Potterton, Roosevelt Park; August 3 2001*

Sex education

Fuck the Catholic bishops — without condoms. — *Pat Hopkins; August 3 2001*

The leading obscenity

When it comes to Aids, the bishops of Southern Africa are right but for the wrong reason: "Catholic bishops on Monday condemned the use of condoms to fight the Aids pandemic gripping the continent, saying it was immoral and dangerous."

Using condoms to fight Aids is indeed immoral and dangerous because condoms don't prevent Aids because Aids is not sexually transmitted. In fact, Aids is not contagious at all. Aids in Africa is just a new name for the diseases of poverty caused by malnutrition, poor sanitation, bad water, parasites and so on. Using condoms to prevent the diseases of poverty is the leading obscenity of our time. — *David Rasnick PhD, member of President Thabo Mbeki's Aids Advisory Panel; August 3 2001*

A CIA conspiracy

Are we to understand from David Rasnick PhD's stance on HIV/Aids that Freddie Mercury and Liberace (to name but two celebrities who succumbed to the dreaded disease) were poor, malnourished, subject to poor sanitation, bad water, parasites and so on? Have we been suckered into thinking otherwise by the mass media, perhaps as part of some elaborate CIA conspiracy? — *Francois Fourie, Bloemfontein; August 17 2001*

NOTES & QUERIES

In Mel Brooks's film *The History of the World: Part I*, Moses is seen dropping a third tablet of stone, so destroying commandments 11 to 15. What might they have been?
● 11. Thou shalt not lie through thy teeth when in government.
12. Musicians, actors and celebrities all count as false gods.
13. Shop on the Sabbath — but remember thy credit limit, and keep it holy.
14. Confession and absolution are not a licence to repeat the sin.
15. Don't believe everything you read. — *Marc Blake, London*

Who is Mr F Moron?

Krisjan Lemmer

Visitors to the www.virusmyth.com website, home on the World Wide Web for those who dispute the link between HIV and Aids, have for some time been greeted by a banner inviting them to "support President Thabo Mbeki and find the truth about Aids". Those who wish to do so can sign a petition, which already includes several loyal followers from South Africa such as journalist and dissident campaigner Anita Allen and her husband Dave, free marketeers Andrew Kenney and Leon Louw, and a less famous individual with a most unlikely moniker. Anyone heard of an Aids dissident called Fucking Moron?

September 15 2000

Shock survey on gay sex

Wilhelm Disbergen

A study of sexual behaviour among gay men in Cape Town — the first of its kind to be conducted in South Africa — has uncovered some shocking results. Despite the incidence of Aids in South Africa, many men are still having unprotected, anonymous sex.

The Triangle Project, a gay and lesbian outreach organisation funded by the Elton John Aids Foundation, asked men at gay venues across Cape Town — widely known as the "gay capital" of South Africa — to complete a questionnaire on their sexual activities. The venues included bars, clubs, steambaths and gay cruising areas in the city and on the Cape Flats. The aim of the survey was to establish the sexual habits and risk-taking among homosexual men — an area that has until now been completely neglected in South African HIV epidemiology.

The survey was "scene" based and this strongly influenced the demographics of the respondents. More than 75% were aged between 20 and 39; and difficulties in accessing informal networks of township-based gay men meant that the respondents were predominantly white (62%, against 25% coloured, 3% Indian and 9% black).

Forty-seven percent of respondents indicated that they were currently in a relationship; but 60% of these had had sex with people other than their partners in the past year. More than half of the men said they had between two and 10 sexual partners in the past 12 months, with 12,7% reporting having had between 20 and 90 sexual partners in the past year.

Only 13% of the men said they had paid for sex in the past year and 17% said they had received money for sex in the same period. When asked whether they had sex with a woman in the past year, 15% of respondents said they had. They were not asked whether this had been safe or unsafe sex.

The men were asked whether they had been tested for HIV and what their HIV status was. The response was that 82% believed they are HIV-negative while 7,7% stated that they believed they were positive. Of the 71% of men who reported having had anal sex in the last year, 25% said they did not use condoms. Two-thirds of the men who did not use condoms said the man they had sex with might have been HIV-positive.

The men were then given a list of 16 environments where they could have had sex recently. Their homes featured prominently (91%); other venues were steambaths (43%), the beach (39%), bars (31%), dark rooms at clubs (25%) and public parks (15%).

The survey suggests a link between public and high-risk sexual behaviour. Men who frequented steambaths and dark rooms were 66% more likely to have had unprotected sex in the past year than those who had sex only at home. Men under the age of 30 were less likely to have had an HIV test than their seniors. A quarter of the men who had between 11 and 20 sexual partners in the past year tested HIV-positive.

The majority of the respondents were consistently protecting themselves, although condom failure (splitting, tearing or slipping off) was reported by 23% at least once in the past year. Most of the men who had HIV tests went after they experienced condom failure. The survey asked the men about their drug use, because it affects high-risk behaviour. Ecstasy, poppers and dagga featured prominently, with recreational drug use most prevalent among the 20 to 29 age group as well as among HIV-positive men. There was a clear correlation between drug use and a higher number of sexual partners. The respondents who used recreational drugs reported condom failure and were three times more likely to have had unprotected sex.

The greater exposure to HIV-infection among young men aged 20 to 29 years was also illustrated in the high number who replied in the affirmative to the question: "I find it hard to say 'No' to sex that I don't want." The survey has concluded that national, provincial and local health funds should be made available to support work being done to prevent the further spread of HIV among gay men.

According to Nigel Crawhall, who is on the board of the Triangle Project, the Department of Health insists that the best statistical method of collating information about HIV prevalence in South Africa remains antenatal sero-prevalence. This is because pregnant women are sexually active, constitute an easily identifiable, accessible and stable population, and are more likely than other groups to be representative of the general population. Because gay men do not attend antenatal clinics, the Department of Health is demonstrating a lack of commitment to inclusion and diversity that could amount to homophobia, Crawhall said.

Annie Leatt, director of the Triangle Project, says the health department is ignoring the prevalence of HIV among gay men and men who have sex with men. She believes HIV prevention should done be in a realistic and non-judgemental way. Asking men to abstain is unrealistic. Safe sex should be eroticised in an effort to make it appealing. Providing condoms and lubicrants in public places does not encourage people to have sex, but provides realistic measures against HIV transmission.

Leatt says safer-sex messages need to be explicit and open with a message that is sex-positive: having sex is not the problem — having unsafe sex is. She said the finding that 12% of gay men had between 20 and 90 sexual partners last year is not unusual: heterosexuals "get up to the same thing". The finding that condom failure was rife probably indicated that these men used government-issue condoms that were all one size, Leatt said. This ignores the fact that penis size varies significantly. Incorrect lubrication could be another reason, as younger gay men were often inexperienced in using lubricants.

Leatt complained that the government did not do enough to address the problems of young, gay men. They are not well-informed and lack both skills and information for HIV prevention.

April 6 2001

How shocked should we be?

Shaun de Waal

One hates to sound like Bill Clinton, but what exactly is meant by "having sex"? The "Shock survey on gay sex" story in last week's *Mail & Guardian* rather blurred the issue — an issue which one suspects remains fuzzy in the minds of many heterosexuals, not just those who are still shocked by the idea that gay men have sex at all.

What does it mean to "have sex"? Heterosexuals are inclined to think of full vaginal/anal penetration as "having sex", and the rest as foreplay. If two men fondle each other in a dark corner of a club, without either reaching orgasm, have they actually had sex? Mutual masturbation may be unprotected sex, but is it unsafe? Is oral sex sex or just playing around?

It's always hard to get one's head around statistics, but these, as presented, seemed especially confusing — and possibly misleading — when read with an uninformed, lazy or prejudiced eye. For a start, the survey represents only men who frequent venues in Cape Town where it is possible to have sex with other men or to pick someone up. Apart from the fact that this does not represent gay men all round South Africa, Cape Town being such a "gay mecca", it does not represent gay men in general. It may show a small percentage, even within the age groups cited — only 185 men were interviewed for the survey. Many gay men find such casual sexual activities distasteful and avoid them like the plague. To speak of "gay sex" as one undifferentiated lump is both insulting and inaccurate.

The survey itself, commissioned by the Triangle Project, is clear about the fact that it is "a first attempt to gain a 'snapshot picture' of this activity" to inform "immediate strategic planning of HIV-prevention initiatives" and to "provide a baseline for future, similar surveys". It includes more detail than was included in the article, obviously, and is clearly of vital importance. But the story does not enable the statistics, as given, to illuminate each other. More than half the men interviewed had sex with up to 10 partners in the past year; on the other hand, 71% had, as the survey itself puts it, "some form of anal intercourse in the last year".

Was that with one partner out of 10? Two? Three? And 25% of those did it unprotected: does that make one fifth of the men interviewed? How do these figures overlap? We have little idea of frequency from the story, though the study itself isolates "at least 23 occasions when men had had unprotected [receptive anal intercourse] that involved potential risk of HIV-transmission".

How shocked should we be? Going beyond the specific remit of the survey, we can ask important questions of both fact and perception, raising issues that need to be investigated more fully (as the survey acknowledges). The results as reported seem to presume a black-and-white difference between safe and unsafe sex. But this is a grey area. For a start, there is no safe sex — only some forms of sex that are safer than others. It's all relative, a continuum, with the degree of risk contingent upon a huge variety of factors, including the viral load borne by an HIV-positive man at the time of sexual activity. We need more information — and the issues raised by the survey need to be opened out, explored further and carefully debated, rather than being presented as simply shocking.

The point by the Triangle Project — that gay men are statistically under-represented in state HIV surveys because they don't attend antenatal clinics, and that there may thus be a "hidden epidemic" of gay HIV/Aids — is valid. But these findings must be placed in context. It seems to be the consensus that in South Africa white (62% of those surveyed) gay men are not a high-risk group — it is black women who are most at risk. If the survey's finding that 7,7% of the men believed they were HIV-positive is reflected in clinical reality, that figure is still lower than the national average for HIV positivity.

How about comparing these statistics to some numbers showing sexual behaviour in the society as a whole? What percentage of heterosexual men have had unsafe sex in the past year? And with how many partners? Without the capacity to place the gay survey statistics in a broader context, it is hard to tell whether the "shock" results are truly worrying or merely the hyperbole of headline writers insensitive to nuance and the fine grain of fact.

The finding that younger gay men are more likely to take sexual risks is sobering; they need urgently to be targeted for education. But then so does the population at large, and, for many, this kind of piece will confuse as much as it clarifies.

April 12 2001

An uncomfortable, unspeakable truth

Sasha Gear

"I don't know if you've seen *Yizo Yizo*?" asks Morris (not his real name), a recently released prisoner who has spent close to three decades in South African prisons. He is explaining how inmates can tell which of the newcomers have been coerced into "Cape Town". "Cape Town" is one of the terms used in prison lingo to refer to anal sex. "Youngsters who have undergone that, they change their style of walking, you saw it in *Yizo Yizo*," he says.

The recent outcry over the screening of a prison rape in *Yizo Yizo* suggests widespread denial about sexual abuse in South African men's prisons. But those who have any knowledge of life in these prisons are only too aware that sexual violence and coercion do occur.

For many, however, these facts represent an uncomfortable, unspeakable truth. *Yizo Yizo* rudely exposed the unspeakable — and provided Morris with a handy way of describing to unversed outsiders the sexual realities in our prisons. More recently the BBC documentary *Cage of Dreams* makes burying our heads in the sands of macho myth more difficult still: viewers hear from the mouths of gang leaders featured on the programme that rape is a gang practice.

Gangs are one of the power-vehicles prisoners use to coerce or persuade others into having sex. Some gangs use gang rape as a recruitment tool and a mode of punishment. Piet, another ex-prisoner and long-standing jail gangster, explains that if, for example, a gang member is caught having sex in a way that contravenes the gang's sex rules — the wrong kind of sex with the wrong kind of person — both parties will be gang-raped. In addition, a prisoner's slot in a gang hierarchy defines his sexual rights. High-ranking members may be entitled to sex, while new recruits and other vulnerables make up the pool of their potential sex slaves.

But coercion is not a constant in sexual interactions in prison, where the blurring of traditional distinctions between consensual and coercive sex is particularly evident. Prison sex ranges from encounters starkly resembling rape to others that appear primarily consensual, with sex serving as a means of exchange. Sex is currency in prison: it may be exchanged for a cigarette or protection from violence and even death.

The dominant forms of sexual relationships among male prisoners closely resemble heterosexual models, and are frequently characterised by ongoing sexual exploitation. Patterns of "man" and "wife" sexual relationships are explicitly provided for in the codes of the 28s gang. They are also apparent, if less explicitly, in gangs such as the Big 5s, the 26s and the Airforce.

These relationships bring with them a set of power relations through which a notion of "manhood" is constructed; and they also determine who has sex with whom. The "man" owns his "wife", who is viewed as his sex slave and servant. In return, the "man" protects and provides his "wife" with material goods. These goods may be small luxuries, or they may be the basic means to survival such as a food ration or a blanket.

Typically, an older prisoner with power in the inmate subculture will take a young and vulnerable prisoner as his "wife". The latter often has little choice about this. The sex act is usually defined as either active or passive, and gender status and identities are accordingly allocated. To be a penetrator makes you a "man". To be penetrated strips you of any claim to "manhood" and turns you into a "woman". This in turn means that rape, and other forms of coercive sex, enable the perpetrator to prove or consolidate his "manhood" by destroying that of his victim.

Often "wives" are initiated into their subordinate role by rape, or fear of rape. Importantly, perpetrators of these acts are overwhelmingly those who consider themselves heterosexual, and who have engaged in heterosexual sex before their incarcerations. Calling these acts "homosexual rape" is therefore inappropriate.

Accounts of prison sex in the United States suggest that dominant prison subcultures do not tolerate people who consider themselves homosexual unless they become substitute women. South African prisons appear to follow suit. It seems too that these subcultures do not tolerate sexual interactions that are not contained within the bounds of the power-defined relationship. For example, "*Uchincha ipondo* [to change a pound]" is when two men express their own sexual desires with each other, taking turns to play the "man". They are usually younger prisoners who are also other men's "wives".

"It's a very big scandal for a young man to do this," Morris says. "It's taken as a very serious matter." If two older men do it, "it's even more scandalous, they can get badly assaulted for that. It's not allowed."

Notions of what it means to be a man together with the power of the inmate subcultures are crucial to understanding how sexual abuses can continue largely unchecked. In prison culture, to inform on fellow prisoners constitutes a heinous crime. The notion that a "real man" cannot be raped also silences most victims. A few will report victimisation when they've been released. But experiences like these are usually a source of such immense humiliation that to talk about them is out of bounds. As the furore around *Yizo Yizo* suggests, the notion that real men cannot be raped is powerful outside prison too.

The prevalence of sexual abuse in prison raises important questions about the welfare of prisoners during their incarceration, and also beyond. Coercive sex in prison is one channel through which particularly destructive notions of masculinity gain momentum. It is also a central contributor to the particularly high risk of HIV transmission in prison.

Given the absence of support for offenders who are brutalised during their incarcerations, among the consequences of their prison experiences are the possibilities of further violence and other forms of abusive and self-destructive behaviour. Since most prisoners are in fact serving fairly short sentences, the brutalities to which they are exposed in prison are likely to be feeding regularly back into society at large. And that should concern all of us.

May 25 2001

NOTES & QUERIES

Is megalomania treatable?
● Never!Never! Ha, ha, ha, ha, ha, ha! — *William Merrin, Wakefield, Yorkshire*

● Megalomania is fully curable. I went for treatment at a small clinic outside Paris and was so impressed with its methods that I started running it, and this is only the beginning. — *David May, London*

● Only by someone with a bigger ego. — *Howard Exton-Smith, Dakar, Senegal*

● Absolutely! I myself have cured more than a million patients single-handedly, using nothing more than the power of my personality and immense intelligence. — *John A Black, Nanaimo, British Columbia, Canada*

Found: Mr Madini

Sipho Madini

If you read *Finding Mr Madini,* or even if you didn't, maybe the reviews caught you. I am Mr Madini, the guy who went missing.

One Sunday I was drunk and walking towards my gontjie, the burrow where I sleep in Braamfontein. To the front stands Wits, tall and erect, the institute of learning. To the left, Saffas the funeral parlour. And every day as I wake and creep out of my gutter; eyes blinking, a kaleidoscope of kids in volksies and GTIs, hearse after hearse, all driving to a luxurious end.

Anyway, walking down this cold and lonely night, as drunk as can be, I stumble across this bunch of matshingilans who just had to make an arrest. For those who are not in the know, matshingilans means security cops. You know, those guys that just stand around really doing nothing. Nothing personal, guys!

Here I come zig-zagging towards this office building that had been broken into and the perpetrators come wooshing past. Only a blur of takkies on the wet pavement, a swoosh and splash as their feet connect with the rain puddles filled only a while ago.

I might look like a pop but I ain't. I cross that place every day of my waking life and I know that place like the back of my hand. The whole kaboom. A police station in front and two behind and teeming with security police. Serious, my bras, I might be stupid but I ain't that stupid. With a white jacket that shines in the dark like a beacon you could see me for miles coming. The ginger sturdy walls of colonial design, the building washing in a flood of light in that far-past-midnight hour. Why would they arrest me? Heaven knows alone. Do they work on a commission basis? Or was it a matter of the damage was done and anyone will do? They are widely reputed to snooze on the job. Enter Malunda — the homeless one. And the rest, as they say, is history.

Next thing I'm in John Vorster with a torn lip, cracked ribs, a busted hand and all bloody. From there to Sun City, where I get herded into a cold shower on a rainy day. While our clothes are being searched, one of the sturdy, short cell owners screams, "*Iphi mali,* you shall take it out," in a demented tone. One chubby fellow gets squealed on. He's got money. Naked and kneeling he is forced to drink bucket after bucket of water.

"*Una manga,* you are lying, that money you'll take it out," comes the promise of the cell owner. Every time the withholder's head rises to protest through a gurgling mouth, a smacking shoe is the answer. Another is being felt through the anus for his hidden currency. "*Skhalo,* I grieve!" screams one of the victims through the window grille in the morning. As a warder passes the dark and grey corridor, "*Voetsek wena!*" is his reply.

I never stay in one cell for too long because I am always on the *jikeleza* (turn), meaning I am always the first one to be chased away when somebody has to go. The total in a cell has to remain constant. But it does not bother me. What scares me is landing up in a certain cell in A2 where its owner Rasta is reported to rape any young man who expects a place to sleep. "What is the warders doing about this?" I ask the young boy next to me. "Nothing as long as he keep paying them," comes the choked reply. Only in Sun City could you as a criminal own a cell or, more frankly, could it be leased to you.

Phaka (meal) time. Stifling heat. Pushing and shoving. One warder with a green, long hosepipe held aloft is chasing a trialist, one who cut into the line. Most people are now reduced to such state. Lack of enough food is called "skepper".

Not enough to feed a little boy, less enough a full-grown man. "Mapapa, food lovers," groans one guy in front of me with disgust. I grunt my agreement and my eyes steal down my now pale and threadworn clothes.

Down the line a trialist is distributing pamphlets. One flutters clumsily out of his hand as he shoves it at the people. "Have you seen this guy?" he demands curtly. He is met by a shake of a head or disinterested stares. A quick glance at his photograph, even I do not recognise this guy. But the text gives my heart a jolt: "MISSING: SIPHO MADINI."

Fok, that's me. I take the pamphlet and shove it in my pocket. "Have you phoned him?" asks one guy stroding down the dark corridor. "Who?" I ask, perplexed.

"That white guy who had come looking for you the other week. Your *ngamula* [boss] man, the one whose number is on the poster. He came here with another picture of him, you and his little daughter."

I palpitate: "Jonathan, I did not know," and return to my cell to think about tomorrow's meeting with my lawyer. After another sleepless night of TV and singing and non-stop fights I am surprised to see that he is a bushy. "You see, *my broer*, plead guilty, that would make things a lot easier," he convinces me with his soft, plumb face. I catch a faint whiff of his French cologne. "But I am innocent. I did not do the crime," I tell him. An immaculate, cultured voice with a hurried expression, he waves away my explanation. "It is just the same or you want to go and sit another six months," he says, eyeglasses clutched in hand.

Ai, these city lawyers drive a hard deal. Now I had been in this spit bucket called Sun City for more than five or six months and, darn, it has a way of wearing you down. Imagine living in constant fear and vigilance, intimidation, beatings and robbing as commonplace as tomorrow itself. People being forced to sing till the early hours of the morning without rest. Songs of rebellion and lamentation. "Hello, darling; come and visit me, I am in jail, I got caught." Over and over, when all you want is desperately to sleep.

"Go and wash these clothes," one boy is commanded as a pile is thrown at his feet. He refuses and a whole gang jumps out of their hidings like a hungry pack of hyenas. Beating him with broomsticks and whatever comes handy. Till he lays still like the death. Every day things are like that.

Sleeping on a cold floor with one blanket and a colony of lice crawling and biting you all over every second of your waking and sleeping life. But still you dare wonder why I pleaded guilty? I didn't expect four years but it was what I got. I was sent ... oops better not to call names, bras, I'd not like to anger them up there, I am goody-goody two shoes now ... let's just say to one of the farm prisons to complete my sentence.

But since then my own story has grown beyond me or about me. Innocent or guilty, it seems not to matter so much. In prison I formed a writing group, by and large with the gentle prodding of my erstwhile mentor and friend, Jonathan Morgan. To utilise my experience I learned from him while writing our first book and to teach my friends in there some writing skills. To give us all a chance to be creative in the place where it is hardest to be just that and to give them a platform to put their voice to paper and bring their experiences to life. For I had come to respect narrative writing and to value its therapeutic side. Giving the inmates a chance to open their souls and heal their wounds. You can even say we had our own mini Truth and Reconciliation Commission. And now I give you a peek into the stories.

In this new book we fell in line with the old book's format, except here I am the front guy and not Jonathan. Standing in front of them, creating an environment where the free flow of ideas is guaranteed and harnessing their creative and narrative skills. With people from different walks of life/cultures telling their own stories/experiences in their own words. From where they were coming to the place we were, conglomerated in prison. By writing into windows affording you, the reader, a glimpse into their life.

Window 1: Where and when; pushing the story back to before he was born.

Window 2: An early childhood memory, and on like that. Written in a bleak surrounding, showing once more the overcoming power of the human spirit.

But unlike its predecessor we had to go ahead in a very underhand fashion to bring it into existence. For fear of interference, and the possibility of censoring. Getting caught might mean a spell in isolation up to 15 days or more. A moving-back of your parole date. For nothing comes out of prison without their express say-so. So at the end of the day it was very cloak-and-dagger stuff.

Six o' clock *folla* time, head counts are being done as we fill into the cell. Seven o' clock *phaka* time, soft porridge and two slice. Eight, job time, for those who refuse, who feel lazy today. Get beaten, manhandled. "You have eaten the food of the jail, you'll work!"

Standing in the cell toilet saunters this impeccably dressed *madala* over to me.

"Look here, gazzie; I will buy you food, dagga, everything," says he smoothly with what is properly his disarming smile. I know what he wants. To be talked to like I'm a woman is not funny. "Fuck you!" is the all-encompassing reply.

I also learn how not to ask for water at the fields in the searing heat. How not to flinch if a thorn pricks my soft hands among the weeds I pull out. A strange vegetable named an eggplant becomes my friend. I hold a milking certificate proudly, although I know I am never going to use it. It is not worth the paper it is written on.

Story meetings are being held in half-empty cells with an eye on the door. And out in the open, with furtive glances over the shoulder. Pieces of papers are being delivered in a slight of the hand. Concealed in socks, innocent-looking books and places better not named for reasons of propriety. Rounded off by poor Jonathan leaving the visiting room with bulges where there were not before and a flushed face in the bargain.

The people who participated in the book come from different parts of the country. From Lesotho to Botswana. The North West to Mpumalanga. Me, I've been all over, but most knew me to begin from the Northern Cape. All coming together one way or another to live in Jozi. Only Rudy of the group having not yet lived there but passing through.

"How about we write a book?" I ask the small group of friends down the almost empty cell. Major, impeccably dressed in his tailored green, smiles enthusiastic. "I had always wanted to write a book." Shorty grins from ear to ear. "Wait, I've written some things," and bursts off to fetch it. Only Sonny looks sceptical at me through hooded eyes, hands in pocket; where he leans on to the double bed.

How did I choose them, or the more appropriate term, how did they choose themselves? First, it was because of their diversity and uniqueness and their willingness to participate. They represent a varied spectrum of the ethnic groups and race here in our beautiful country. And some of them the different gangs in prison. Like 26s, whose main oath is money and the smoking of dagga.

Big 5s, who believe in close cooperation with the authorities, literally translated squealing, just to name a few. For you could not purport to write about prison without including the gangs, for they are an integral part of prison life.

The stories they got to tell are nail-biting, riveting, humorous. And others just plain astounding. There is David, the country-bumpkin meets Big City. He came to Jozi to work the mines like his father before him and instead found himself abducted by his fellow countrymen, to join the Amarashiyans — a traditional Sotho gang more known for their blankets. David's stories are like paintings in the sky, an eye for detail, that you can almost smell the taste of grass and hear the rustle of the river there in his hometown Lesotho.

Shorty, the skew-eyed little devil with a jolt in his step, who is in jail "*vir staan en kyk*". His stories are funny if not sad. A real ladies' man with a twist. Sonny, a 26 from Eldos who single-handedly vanquished a gang, which bothered him too much! His story to look out for: *Sonny: Tant' Sannie and the Spices*! Deon, the sweet-faced Mpumalanger, who if he don't find something that is intelligent in your house might just trash your place. And Rudy, our white golden boy with a psycho temper.

Their stories are told behind a grim background where everything is not a right but a privilege. Where things they have taken for granted suddenly rears their importance. And where you suddenly realise, like a nagging toothache, that your life is no more in your own hands but somebody else's (warders and all that cabal). The word that sums it all up comes from Rudy: "*Tronk is 'n kak plek, my broer!*"

But they managed to pick their own stories up and look behind their bleak surroundings. To a fresher start and life behind crime. Sonny has decided to open up a pavement restaurant in Industria selling *pap en vleis* after his release. Rudy: "I'm going to design a simple machine that fix water-pipes. It's gonna be a money spinner, you'll see!" Shorty, proudly holding a church certificate aloft: "I am going to be a preacher outside, you just wait and see, you just wait!"

This book is not just statistics in *The Citizen* or victim stories, it is from both sides. Why a cute little baby loved by everybody today belongs to the most loathed section of our population. It is also not a book to justify them or be analytic. It is just to give you, the reader, a glimpse into the other side. And now we are looking for a publisher to make their effort into a book and our dreams into a reality. For if it hits the bookshelves it promises to be a very revealing, gripping, page-turning book.

December 1 2000

The writing of desire

Antjie Krog

"I had almost completed *The Rights of Desire* when *Disgrace* was published. Despite some problems I had with the book, I was in real awe! I knew that in many ways it would have a definitive influence on South African writing and was faced with a serious difficulty. I needed a violent action to break through the protective mould of my main character and had planned a rape scene. Then came *Disgrace* and I was forced to change the story. In a way it was a good thing, because my text gained a lot from the new direction."

In his latest book, André Brink chose to interact directly with JM Coetzee's *Disgrace*. He takes as his theme Professor David Lurie's defence after being accused of sexual misconduct with a student: "I rest my case on the rights of desire ... on the god who makes even the small birds quiver."

For many Afrikaans readers Brink has always been an enigma. When he emerged as one of the Sestigers (a literary movement of the 1960s) with outrageous ideas and razor-sharp attacks on the Afrikaner establishment, people were confused. On the face of it he was an *"ordentlike man"*, a *Boereseun* from a magistrate's household; the eldest of four children, he obtained the highest matric marks in the Transvaal. It was also known that at the age of 12 he had submitted a novel for publication, patiently typed for him by his father. When he was 14 his first full-length "adult" novel was rejected because it was too erotic.

"Ever since I was nine I knew that I would be a writer. I knew that I live through words." He wandered about the garden at Jagersfontein talking to himself in English. "I could hardly speak English, but with hindsight I suppose it was a desire to find a kind of private space reachable only through a language which sounds different from everyday talk."

The Brinks were a family of voracious readers. "Whenever we met after being apart for a year or so we would greet and talk, happy to be together. But within half an hour each of us would be alone in a quiet spot, reading." Brink's mother published books for children; his sister, Elsabé Steenberg, was a prominent author of books for teenagers. "But my father could have been a writer. On long winter evenings I would declare a match between my parents, give them a theme, and they'd have to come up with a story. Time and again my father astounded us."

The story of *The Rights of Desire* (*Donkermaan* is the Afrikaans title) announced itself one night on a flight between London and South Africa. "I was hyper-conscious that I was near my retiring year and that things were becoming countable [*telbaar*]. A writer seldom writes after the age of 80 and it was a terrible thought: fewer books perhaps left to write than I have fingers on my hand. I went into a complete panic about being old and redundant and useless. That night everything crystallised."

Since *Die Ambassadeur,* the book which put Brink on the Afrikaans map as a writer of remarkable calibre, he had wanted to explore the relationship between an older man and a much younger woman. For this he needed a lot more maturity. On the plane he knew the time had come. And then there was Antje of Bengal, a ghost haunting the Paapenboom Road house in *The Rights of Desire*. Brink is known for using suppressed parts of South African history in his work, from slave rebellions to the life of Bram Fischer. When he first wrote about Fischer in *Gerugte van Reën,* the imprisoned communist could not be quoted, but through that novel readers became familiar with his background.

After initially wanting to stay in France ("I was ashamed of South Africa, I was embarrassed by the Afrikaner"), he returned here and wrote his infamous *Kennis van die Aand* (*Looking on Darkness*), one of the first Afrikaans books to be banned in South Africa. In an act as courageous as it was politically incorrect, Brink made his main character and narrator a coloured man. I remember that in Kroonstad my mother was the only person who already had a copy when it was banned. The dominees of the dorp decided they had to read the book in order to guide their flock, so my mother was phoned. I have it in my possession, still in the brown paper cover used to disguise it.

In my personal experience this is one book of which black and white Afrikaans readers have said that it changed their lives in a fundamental way. Afrikaners found themselves for the first time identifying with someone of another colour. Black people said: When I read this book I realised that whites are beatable, that we could force them to accept that we are like them.

Brink also introduced a specifically African magic realism (distinct from the Latin-American variety) into Afrikaans. His favourite authors in this regard are Zakes Mda and Amos Tutuola — especially the latter's *My Life in the Bush of Ghosts* and *The Palm-Wine Drinkard.* "We are so fortunate in South Africa ... the stories I heard from the Basotho woman who raised me, the Hottentot cosmology, the whole stream of Afrikaans *'spookstories en goëlery'.* I'd say that the important difference between African magic realism and that of other continents is that it has this link with the forefathers, it directly influences how we live with one another."

Both *The Rights of Desire* and *Disgrace* deal with an ageing white man within a fast-changing South Africa. Each is introduced to this new world by a white woman. Each finds the situation in which he has to live unbearable. Yet the two protagonists differ widely. Brink's character experiences his redundancy together with the formidable coloured woman who works for him; in many ways the two of them represent the most threatened of groups: white men and coloured women.

Moreover Brink's character has a struggle history, as he and his wife Magrieta resisted the District Six removals. While Coetzee's Professor Lurie is trying to write an opera on Byron, Brink's Ruben is looking for memory in the remains of the slave woman. One might say that Brink's book represents an Afrikaner take on the new South Africa, while Coetzee's character functions more in an English South African milieu.

Brink has never been as popular among members of the Afrikaans literary establishment as one might think. Each time he applied for an Afrikaans professorship he was turned down in favour of a lesser candidate but a better Broeder. So he was always teaching Afrikaans at English universities. He is notable among the Sestigers for having received hardly any literary recognition for his novels. Despite international acclaim and prizes, he has yet to gain the Hertzog Prize for prose. By comparison fellow Afrikaner establishment-basher Breyten Breytenbach has been profusely honoured in Afrikaans.

Add to this the fact that no other figure in Afrikaans literature has been quite so prolific in so many genres. Apart from his 20-odd novels (of which *Lobola vir die Lewe* and *Orgie* brought about a radical stylistic shift in Afrikaans writing during the 1960s), Brink has written some 10 plays and translated even more, all of them successfully performed, as well as a range of travel books. His extensive reading has enabled him to explain every new direction in Afrikaans literature, through articles, letters, essays, reviews or lectures. He was prominent in the fight against censorship. His firm grasp of world literature meant that for decades he helped steer Afrikaans writing on an interesting and healthy course by way of reviews in the Afrikaans Sunday newspapers. He is the author of books on brandy and dessert wine. He used to write a weekly humour column, and has translated countless classics from the several languages he speaks, among them works for children such as *The Little Prince* and *King Arthur*.

Brink's main character ponders on the "rights of desire": "If I claim desire as my right and its nature lies in motion, its motion towards the other, does not my right to desire invoke the right of other to refuse me? But only if 'I am' in this equation becomes wholly conditional upon 'You are'. And where does that leave desire?" Brink himself says of Ruben that he "becomes conscious of a country full of people with desires on many different levels. In the course of the story he learns that desire isn't all about fulfilment. It has a broader context. Desire consists not in being in possession of the other, but in an awareness of others, in a humane way of behaving towards others. Through his desire he has developed a conscience."

I ask him about what for me is the most beautiful part in the book: the discovery of the remains of the slave woman under the house. Brink looks at me: "I was so surprised when that happened! It was so unexpected that I was initially dumbfounded." Now it is my turn to be amazed: "But you wrote the book! How could you be surprised?" He smiles, somewhat embarrassed. "This is why one writes. For that moment that no planning, no structure, no skill can foresee ... That moment when one looks in utter astonishment at what one has written."

Brink confesses to being an obsessive planner and notekeeper. He makes notes of things he reads, hears and thinks, even while working on a particular book, in order to be able to return to sub-themes later. A story usually begins with an incident or a place. Then he plans the whole narrative — every character, every detail — on the tacit understanding that he may not stick to it at all. "If by the end of the first chapter I am still with my original plan, then I am worried."

When he is into a story he writes morning, noon and night. Since he started to translate *Kennis van die Aand* in an attempt to bypass the ban on the book, Brink works in both Afrikaans and English. (Word has it that he once had to sign a divorce settlement barring him from publishing in Afrikaans anything dealing with the break-up of his marriage or his relationship with a younger woman. The subsequent book appeared only in English).

"Working in two languages means I write a novel twice. Usually I write in Afrikaans and afterwards find, while translating, that it takes a different route because I notice other things, so I go back and work it into the Afrikaans ... sometimes things are such that they only work in one language. For instance, Magrieta can only exist fully in Afrikaans. Also Tessa uses a specific English-cluttered Afrikaans" (a kind of crossover language that opens up the possibility of her leaving the protagonist for a young black man). With *The Rights of Desire,* Brink started in English. "The main character was so close to myself that I deliberately used English to get him on his feet as an entity, before I could allow him into Afrikaans."

To what extent is this novel part of a new kind of South African band-wagon? Stories about crime, affirmative action, black thugs and fearful whites, which do well precisely because they play on the Afro-pessimism of many readers?

"I would say that my book ends very positively. Living here has taught Ruben to live responsibly with others." The story has less to do with race than with the fear of remaining selfish, becoming old and redundant.

Although Brink is intensely private and always charmingly *ordentlik,* there are some wonderful Brink tales in circulation. Like the one about him and his wife Marisa raising a little black girl. One day Brink takes her to the crèche and, as they enter hand in hand, her friend asks: "Is this your daddy?" Emphatically the child replies: "No, he's not my daddy, he's my nanny!"

August 25 2000

The ladies' gold medal for drivel

David Beresford

"I have come to the conclusion that I must be a selfish, unsympathetic, disgusting so and so." — Noeleen Maholwana Sangqu, news editor, Radio 702

It is said by many a veteran journalist that once one gets the intro (introductory paragraph) right, the rest is easy. The same is true, no doubt, of the consequences if one gets the intro wrong, and there can be few better examples of it than the above quotation, the first sentence of a column written by the broadcaster, Noeleen Maholwana Sangqu, in *The Citizen* last week.

Nobody, not even the news editor at Radio 702, proclaims themselves to be "selfish", "unsympathetic" and "disgusting" in anticipation of being believed. Which reduces her observation to the disingenuous, resort to which is, in boxing parlance, leading with the chin. I therefore turned to the letters page of the following day's *Citizen* prepared to wince at the sight of Sangqu, metaphorically at least, splattered across the canvass. To my surprise there was only one solitary attack on her, a flurry of ill-directed blows by an indignant correspondent which Sangqu will no doubt have little difficulty in ignoring.

Which, when you consider it, is astonishing. Imagine the fuss if someone had written something in this day and age along the lines of: "I feel sorry for blacks ... Blacks do not look good and that is a fact ... I know I should not be feeling this way. It is politically incorrect. They are human just like you and me. After all, everyone is equal, no matter what their physical appearance. But this is not the way I feel ... if you really think about it you probably feel the same ..."

Sangqu's confusion of feelings did not arise, at least in this instance, from racial bigotry and her column made no reference to pigmentation, white or black. Her confession stemmed from the sight of "blind, limbless human beings parading their skills at the Paralympic Games in Sydney". In other words the lot to whose presence she objects are not "whites", or "blacks", but the so-called "disabled" who are identifiable, not by degrees of pigmentation, but their shortage of limbs and/or tendency to walk into lamp posts in the middle of the day.

It just so happens that I have long shared an element of her prejudice, although hopefully mine is one marked by less confusion and is directed indiscriminately towards the Olympic movement in general, rather than specifically towards the Paralympics. It is a prejudice born of a pastime known on my school athletics field as "the hop, step and jump". This athletics event I found irritating beyond belief, because of the question it left eternally unanswered: Why? Why not the ... well, the hop-skip-jump-bend-over-and-blow-a-raspberry-through-your-legs-at-the-silly-buggers-watching event? That would be a better test of dexterity, at least, not to mention theatrical ability.

The elevation of the hop-step-and-jump to Olympian dignity, as the "triple jump", has coloured my adult view of "the Games" which I have never been able to take seriously as a result. I can understand a curiosity to find the fastest runner in the world, or the greatest jumper, or the best fighter, or the strongest person — all as part of a tradition, as a hangover from the need to find "champions" for the battlefield in days before gunpowder (or was it the longbow?) rendered all combatants roughly equal in the lottery of distant death which is modern warfare.

But the rationalisation begins to break down after that, with the introduction of qualifications. The greatest leaper ... with a hop and a skip and a jump. The fastest runner ... who is female. The best fighter ... who is a lightweight. The small-guy-best-able-to-pick-up-with-two-motions-heavy-objects-stuck-at-either-end-of-a-bar. Logically the trend would soon make a complete nonsense of the Games — high jump for the shorter-legged, perhaps, or the featherweight women's shot put. Why would the short-legged want to leap high in the air, any more than a petite woman would want to hurl lumps of iron around the place?

Just such a nonsense underlaid — it seemed to me — the motivation for the Paralympics. Why would a legless man want to compete in the marathon, or throw the javelin? Why not something more in line with their strengths — night-time boxing without lights, if they have to, where the blind would have a "natural" advantage. Or arm-wrestling, in which the upper-body strength natural to the paraplegic would no doubt triumph.

For a while I toyed with the idea that this confusion of athletics was one big practical joke on the world, presumably devised by some mad Aussie television mogul at a loss as to how otherwise to amuse himself. That suspicion was prompted by one Olympic event which caught my eye by accident while flicking through television channels — what can best be described as "the suspending herself upside down in a swimming pool and wriggling her toes in the air in a meaningful sort of a way" event. It struck me as an obvious case of mental ... well, sort of disablement.

But then it struck me that the key to all the confusion is the very word "disabled", so unfortunately enshrined in the anti-discrimination clauses of the Constitution. To disable is to render non-functional, to disqualify. One is only disabled when one is dead. "Handicapped" might seem a better word, but handicapped for what? The term can only be used broadly, because the truth is we are all "handicapped" in one way or another. I would be handicapped in most countries in the world by my stupidly monolinguistic mind, but among English-speaking peoples I get by okay (albeit with a dictionary as a crutch). A pregnant woman would be handicapped in women's weightlifting, but is otherwise self-evidently enabled and advantaged. It would be silly to describe as handicapped a man as distinguished, brilliant and presumably wealthy as Stephen Hawking, unless it was in the hop, step and jump category.

Not only birth, accident, but the very act of training for advantage in one activity might handicap one in another direction. The heavyweight weight-lifter guzzling T-bone steaks, for example, may be physically handicapped in the high jump — or, for that matter, pot-holing, or prancing down a Milan catwalk in hot-pants. This train of thought leads me to the conclusion that the Olympics and the Paralympics (which, significantly, are now to be combined) are not motivated by a mad comic genius, as I suspected, but a benevolent philanthropist with a gentle sense of humour who is determined to confront us all with the fertility of our contradictions.

So roll up, roll up, gentle folk. It is time for the launch of the Anything-goes Olympics. And if someone would care to strike up the national anthem I will take this opportunity to present Noeleen Maholwana Sangqu with her richly deserved gold medal in the drivelling-on-in-a-vacuous-sort-of-way event.

November 3 2000

Paralympian athletes go on push for pain

Neal Collins

While drugs may be the scourge of the Olympics, officials monitoring the Paralympics have a very different problem: they have to go in search of pain. Contestants this week blew the whistle on what has now become an open secret in the world of disabled sport. Many disabled athletes — some suggest nine out of 10 — practise "automatic dysreflexia" or boosting.

This is the process where disabled athletes break their own bones or nail their private parts to the wheelchair in an effort to increase their performance. They cannot feel the physical pain as these parts of their bodies are numb. But their body still "feels" the damage and "boosts" the level of performances through adrenaline rushes that enhance performance just as surely as nandrolone or testosterone. Tanni Grey-Thompson, a British wheelchair racer who has been the star of several Paralympic games, says: "We have to find a test for boosting or it will become as big a problem as drugs in the ordinary Olympics."

Some examples of boosting from Paralympians include breaking their own legs and toes; driving nails into their testicles; twisting their scrotums and sitting on them; drinking large amounts of water and then pegging their catheters so their bladders fill to bursting point. The "pain stimulus" creates an adrenaline-like substance called noradenlin, which ups the heart rate and raises blood pressure, which in turn enhances the ability to exercise more strongly.

Sources say that up to nine out of 10 quadraplegic and paraplegic athletes try it — and as yet it can't be detected by dope testers. One British athlete is quoted as saying: "I began 'boosting' about 18 months ago. I had heard about it from some of the other racers on the international scene. Quite a lot of people seemed to be doing it and saying it was safe and had improved their times. I thought it was worth a try to see if it worked for me as well. It didn't involve taking any drugs and that was good." Autonomic dysreflexia can lead to a heart attack or stroke.

None of the bodies governing disabled sport know if "boosting" really works, but it has been given credence by a survey carried out in 1994 by a team of Canadian doctors, who published their work in the *Clinical Journal of Sports Medicine*. Their results showed that "boosting" impoved race times by about 10%. Dr Gary Wheeler, who wrote the report, said: "That means that in a marathon one of the top disabled athletes could better his or her performance by about 12 minutes."

But Wheeler emphasised that the procedure does not come without its costs. He said: "We also found alarming rises in blood pressure, twice as high as those we'd normally find during exercise — readings just below the point at which a body would usually give out. The athletes we studied told us they felt they could control it. But because of the sometimes unreliable nature of the body, the way it reacts differently to different surroundings and events, we just don't know that it is possible to manage 100% of the time."

Autonomic dysreflexia has not yet claimed the lives of any disabled sportsmen, although in a non-sporting context, deaths, brain haemorrhages, strokes and heart attacks have been reported from those quadriplegics in whom it occurs naturally. It is the possibility of such a tragedy on a sports field that has attracted the attention of the International Paralympic Committee. Grey-Thompson, winner of three golds so far in Sydney, says: "It's vitally important the authorities find a way of testing for 'boosting', and soon. Otherwise I think it could develop in the way that anabolic steroids have in able-bodied sport. If people don't know fully the implications of what they are doing and make a mistake, someone could die."

October 27 2000

NOTES & QUERIES

Since musicians never stop composing, will there ever be a time when it is impossible to produce an original tune?

● Twenty minutes' exposure to your local radio station might convince you that it has already become impossible to produce an original tune. The new technology of drum machines and software programs that write songs for you has ensured that the points of reference for young songwriters become fewer with every passing hit parade. An ability to understand the structures of music or compose a lyric that avoids banality in every meter is no longer necessary to come up with a "song" — record it at home, get it on the radio and cover yourself in writhing blonde groupies as the money rolls in. — *Peter LeRoy, Malmesbury*

● This question confuses musicianship with the act of composition, and it deals superficially with the profound issue, namely originality. The great majority of musicians play music composed by others. Very few musicians are themselves composers, though they may fancy it otherwise. Original "tunes" are never "produced". Rather, the act of creating an original work of music inexorably and inevitably involves the composer with the medium by which the music is inspired within the composer's heart, whether we term this medium The Muse, The Spirits or God. True inspiration in music, as in dreams, never comes in the form of a copy. Therefore there will never be a time when it is impossible for original music to be created. With modern music, particularly "popular" music, so full of trivial "copies", you just have to look a little harder for it. — *Maestro Robert Maxym, composer and conductor*

● Yes. Precious few real tunes are being written now, at least ones that would register as such to a Schubert or a Gershwin. Plenty of people nowadays consider any collection of successive sounds a tune. That would not fit the *Oxford Dictionary*'s definition: "Arrangement of single notes in musically expressive succession." Some believe the slightest variation of a "tune" creates a new "tune". By that criterion we could call out, "new tune!" whenever a singer missed a top note. As our societies become more and more dominated by visual information and suffer increasing musical background noise (the "devaluation of sound" noted by many a historian) it is only a matter of time before tunes will not only cease to be written, but almost cease to exist altogether. Only in musty electronic libraries will tunes survive, but nobody will hear them, because by then they will be incomprehensible. — *David Stanhope, Sydney, Australia*

● It's already happened. After the 1970s we just got rehashes. — *Martin Connolly, Isehara, Japan*

Another day, another dolour

Robert Kirby

I t's hard not to be cynical about the media response to the fatalities at Ellis Park last week. Print was bad enough, but South African television once again showed itself up as an institution almost completely devoid of dignity or restraint. I am sure that in the television newsrooms they hang a devil's purse of sentimental clichés, cheap overstatement and gushy hyperbole, to be dipped into whenever deemed necessary by the editors.

It's also hard to determine which was worse, e.tv or the SABC, as their reporters and newswriters luxuriated in melodramatic embellishment of anything they could lay their hands on. I'll plump for the SABC if only because of an inclusion in a news bulletin of the following evening.

Now there's nothing that stimulates the average SABC or e.tv cameraman more than getting close-ups of the grieving relatives of crime or calamity's victims. But this time the SABC outdid even its own putrid norms.

A man came out of a mortuary, his face in shocked grief. He had just identified his dead wife. Does the SABC acknowledge that vehement personal emotion of this kind is not material for its screens and that to film someone in a state such as this man's is the grossest invasion of his privacy? Of course not. What the SABC did was to shove a camera in the man's face for about a minute, as he whipped and writhed in his distress. Then, as if that wasn't enough, the SABC broadcast the thing.

What brute's mentality prevails at the SABC news department, which sanctions, if not encourages, its repertoire of polluting journalism? It's not that this was a one-off. The SABC and e.tv daily exhibit their pornotropic fascination with murder's bloodstains and their lingering inspections of motor accidents. They are both of contaminated tabloid pedigree.

A hastily convened press conference on the Ellis Park disaster was held on the Thursday afternoon and transmitted live. Notwithstanding the technical fiasco of faulty microphones and sloppy direction, this gave us a front-row view of the hypocrisy behind all the wailing and gnashing of teeth.

About 10 administrators and politicians were lined up, not one of them missing this God-given opportunity to express his or her personal anguish. Underneath all the bale and sorrow it was easy to smell the bilge: they were actually there to get in some early and energetic passing of the buck. Despite its shrillness, the grief was entirely secondary to smug alibi.

Most bogus of the lot was soccer mandarin Robin Petersen, who took it upon himself to deliver an oily little sermon to the journalists, telling them to be suitable to the tragedy — that's when he wasn't interrupting anyone daring to ask a penetrating question.

The catchphrase which was to adorn television screens and newspaper posters for the first few days was that reliable old standby: A Nation Mourns. Those who brandished it must be well out of touch. The predominant public emotion arising from the Ellis Park deaths was far less one of grief than of anger, of outrage that it had been allowed to happen.

The whole awful business was rounded off last Sunday with a so-called "cleansing" ceremony held at Ellis Park. As expected all the dignitaries were there to be seen, and what little I watched seemed to be done with some reserve — I specifically exclude Don Mattera's quite appalling alliterative poem. What did strike me as contradictory was the fact that they don't regularly hold these sort of ceremonies for the legions of other casualties in our happy new democracy. When it comes to violent and unnecessary deaths, the Easter weekend's road toll was far in excess of the Ellis Park numbers. Do, say, the 30 dead in a bus crash not qualify for national lament? For that matter, the hundreds of thousands of the murdered, the tens of thousands of babies born with HIV, casualties of an indifferent government? Or is public grief doled out only on the basis of its political marketability?

April 20 2001

LETTERS

Ethnick cleansing

The *Mail & Guardian* remains my favourite ethnic newspaper. I was interested to read your valiant defence of that outstanding "English" coach, Nick Mallett, with his "refreshing" command of the global tongue. Sadly, he seems to have been ethnically cleansed from his position in a dark and execrable conspiracy mounted by the South African Rugby Football Union and influential sportswriters from Afrikaans newspapers.

How on earth did the Springboks win a match — let alone the Rugby World Cup — before they had a *rooinek* coach? A naive believer in rainbow-nation theory, I was unaware that these categories applied to rugby, until I heard the great Mr Mallett speak at a captain's dinner at the Dainfern Golf Club two years ago.

Mr Mallett's speech was liberally sprinkled with anti-Afrikaans ethnic slurs such as "Dutchman", "rocks", etc, and he expounded an amazing theory of Springbok excellence. He said the national team was so good because it contained Afrikaners who were stupidly fearless and therefore "tackled like hell", whereas the Englishmen provided strategy. The Dutchman-Rooinek combination was therefore a near invincible one of pure brawn plus pure brain.

Not being a connoisseur of rugby, I subsequently tried to apply this theory in watching the team on the field. Somehow the ones with less fresh English accents, such as Joost van der Westhuizen, did a lot of clever things with the ball while Percy Montgomery and Bobby Skinstad appeared inhibited by their superior intelligence and kicked or threw good ball away.

After hearing Mallett, the thought did cross my mind of how a coach with such firm views on the cognitive abilities of what used to be called the "two white races" could hold the national team together. It also occurred to me that, given the all-white team during his tenure, Mr Mallett might be a secret reader of *The Bell Curve* and an adherent of the belief in an "intellectual elite" that is no doubt white and Anglo-Saxon. — *Dan Roodt, Dainfern; November 3 2000*

Women! Out of the ring (into the kitchen)

The age of decadence has descended upon us with a vengeance. I refer to women pugilists bashing each other senseless.

The terms of the South African Boxing Bill that Minister of Sport and Recreation Ngconde Balfour will table provide for women to participate in boxing. It seems that Western civilisation depends for its amusement on ever-increasing depravity to satisfy hedonistic debauched desires. The dignities of the past are mocked by the vulgarities of the present.

Women should stay out of the ring as they could be subjected to untimely menstruation if a blow upsets the rhythm of ovulation. Women pugilists would turn the ring into a squawking, cackling gymnasium of dishonour. Over and above the gloves, will they be issued deodorants and tampons as well as gum-guards? Will they be issued special bras to hold the boobs in place? What of a blow to the boobs? It could cause incipient cancer.

When entertainment becomes a Roman circus of women bashing the daylights out of each other, then society becomes inane spectators and its amusements a spectacular farce. Such a nation finds itself at great risk of cultural and moral decline. — *Clive Percival, Benmore; March 23 2001*

The last outpost

Bryan Rostron

Cape Town, appended like an afterthought on the southern tip of Africa, still doesn't quite know where it fits into the modern map of the world. When marketing itself for tourism or promoting a self-image, the city repeats what it has done for the past 349 years: it gazes abroad and continues to imagine that it's a European outpost. Cape Town thus retains a curiously semi-detached relationship with the continent to which it is, however precariously, attached.

Cape Town's new unicity administration seems intent on perpetuating this centuries-old fantasy. While boasting that it is an international tourist destination and a world-class city, the illusion is sustained by the same expedient that the city fathers have resorted to since the arrival of Jan van Riebeeck. They try to sweep the natives out of sight.

The latest manifestation of this old colonial illusion is the recently announced "Operation Shack Attack", a plan to remove the shambolic shack settlements that are the very first sight to greet foreign visitors as they leave Cape Town International airport. This idea has been harshly criticised as being motivated more by a desire to remove an eyesore than to deal with the underlying problem. Recently, with much fanfare, the premier of the Western Cape proclaimed a clampdown on vendors plying their trade at traffic lights. Also to be removed: the otherwise unemployed sellers of *The Big Issue* magazine.

Yet this sweeping-away of African realities is a conjuring trick that not even the fanatical iron fist of apartheid could sustain. The result is that Cape Town today remains a city of exclusions, not inclusions. "Returning to live here after an absence of more than 15 years in Gauteng has given me a horrible sense of having gone backwards in time," says a white woman friend of mine. "Cape Town today is more polarised and separate than it was in the Eighties. It is a city with a collection of the most extraordinary pockets of people all living in their own little worlds — and never the twain shall meet. Many cities in the world have disparate communities — New York, for example. But what differs is that New Yorkers consider themselves and 'those others' to be New Yorkers. In Cape Town, certain pockets of people define themselves as Capetonians and the rest ... well, they're just the rest."

Black professionals I have spoken to strongly feel that Cape Town is in a time warp. This, of course, has long been the city's charm to many whites and foreign visitors.

The complexity of Cape Town, and its fascination, is that it is indeed a rainbow city: white, black, coloured, Muslim and Indian. But here the colours in the rainbow, as opposed to Desmond Tutu's intended symbolism, seldom mix. They remain starkly separated, as often as not by railway lines: the grids of exclusion seem as rigid as ever. Thus when Cape Town promotes its self-image as a "world-class" city, it is repeating a pattern reflected in early colonial maps and paintings: the untidy settlement presented itself as an ordered European hamlet with no locals in sight.

Today Cape Town is obsessed with tourism, the Holy Grail of all modern metropolitan marketing. Yet this imperative means, once more, an overriding concern about how the city will appear to outsiders, rather than what it's like for the majority of its inhabitants to live there. "Look, tourism creates jobs!" a white promotions expert scolded me. "In the real world, you have to market yourself."

The real world? Tourism is mostly about conjuring glossy images and fulfilling usually clichéd expectations; it is about escaping from daily routine ("the real world") into a vacation fantasy. The purple prose of tourist brochures does not reflect the "real" city: hence the logic behind "Operation Shack Attack".

Today, as the plane circles the city, the tannoy will draw a visitor's attention to the magnificent sight of Table Mountain, not to that equally astonishing apparition: the glinting grey sea of shacks stretching out over the sandy wastes of the Cape Flats like some huge medieval encampment of a rag-tag army besieging a shining city centre.

As soon as visitors exit the airport, they see nothing but shacks packed along both sides of the N2 into the city. Some of these shacks are built on an old rubbish dump. The visitor speeds along the highway towards Kaapstad, undoubtedly unaware of the extra patrols now assigned to this stretch of road because of the spate of attacks, including a recent murder, on motorists whose cars break down.

To the right, just after the black township of Langa, are the huge twin pepper pots of Athlone Power station.

Like most of the city's white residents, our visitor will almost certainly have missed one of the most fascinating sights in the whole city, a juxtaposition that expresses a social complexity so often denied here. In the field next to the power station, in the shadow of those ugly concrete cathedrals to modern science, are makeshift plastic bomas for the seclusion of *abakweta*, Xhosa youths undergoing initiation.

Ahead is Table Mountain. It is a titanic marker, appearing even in my dreams. The mountain bears an uncanny resemblance, both in appearance and location, to a description by Dante of the terrestrial paradise, 150 years before the Portuguese ever set eyes on it. Many early travellers' accounts describe the mountain, and the Cape, as a Garden of Eden. Such lyrical prose has an uncanny echo in our modern tourist brochures.

Today, however, such elegiac descriptions startlingly deny the evidence of our own eyes: the panorama, in all its splendour and squalor, from the summit of Table Mountain. Most of the city's population still live beyond the European pale and that vast shanty encampment now stretches all the way across the peninsula to the Indian Ocean.

And out there in the bay is Robben Island, which for years under apartheid was actually airbrushed out of postcards and official pictures of this supposedly sylvan scene. So what, when we talk of "Cape Town", are we erasing from the picture now?

Despite feeling slightly bilious after reading the overwrought prose of several tourist brochures, I was at my desk trying to decide how to convey my own deep affection for this complex city when my phone rang. It was a (white) friend of mine, very distressed. The previous evening she had taken her 12-year-old son and his Zimbabwean friend out for a meal in the centre of Cape Town, when the owner of a restaurant near Long Street had stormed out cracking a sjambok.

"My son had a hood over his head, so this man obviously thought that here were two black street children," said my friend. "He grabbed them, shook them, hit my son — then was shocked when he realised he was white. But when I went into the restaurant to remonstrate, the white patrons at the bar were very abusive. The informal parking attendant in the street told me that they sjambok the street kids regularly."

Jakes Jacobs, a seasoned "street worker" from The Homestead, which operates a network of projects for the city's street children, visited the restaurant. "The manager admits he came out with a sjambok, but says he didn't hit the children, only a table," says Jacobs, who has worked with street kids for 16 years. "Then he saw it was a white child and got a fright. I gave him my card and told him to let us deal with the kids in the future and that if we had another complaint we'd take the appropriate steps."

Jacobs says he regularly deals with such incidents. There is a drive on to smarten up the city centre, to crack down on crime and remove the homeless. Street children are frequently, and wrongly, made the scapegoats for crime. A former mayor of Cape Town described them as "marauding hordes of feral children". The city's new Democratic Alliance mayor, Peter Marais, visited The Homestead "Drop-In" centre shortly before the recent unicity elections and stunned staff by saying he wasn't surprised that the street kids didn't want to go home because of all the "luxury". When challenged to explain what he meant by luxury, Marais said: "Running water and sewerage. They don't have that where they come from."

When opening this drop-in centre last year, Minister of Education Kadar Asmal put his finger on the problem. "What do we see when we look at street children? Do we see dirty, smelly, glue sniffing, thieving delinquents — or do we see children whose constitutional rights to shelter, food and education have been impaired?" he asked. "Yet there are so many in our country who adopt a "not-in-my-backyard" approach ... a belief that you can get rid of a problem through heavy-handed programmes, which simply remove problems from the public eye and then everyone can pretend they don't exist. It is a middle-class dream: make it invisible and the problem will disappear!"

This still seems to be the attitude of Cape Town's administrators and business leaders. In trying to present a First World face to the world, they are simply denying the facts: the very existence of the majority of the city's population. Hence that prevailing sense of siege and the response: sweep the unwashed masses back to from whence they came. Annette Cockburn, the feisty director of The Homestead, says bluntly: "Frankly, I get a sense in Cape Town that we are going backwards. I'm completely disillusioned with local government. New councillors come in and say 'we must do something about the homeless' and then produce policy documents. It's policy, policy, policy and little action."

On the morning that I visited the Yizani "Drop-In" Centre near the hub of the city, about 20 children had come in off the streets to play for a few hours and to eat. One child was missing a leg, others had bruises and bandages. The majority of these children are "daytime strollers", who come into town to beg, then go home at night; only about a quarter actually live on the streets.

The Homestead has seven centres across Cape Town, including residential care, educational facilities and work projects for parents. The children are treated with care, love, gusto and a refreshing lack of sentimentality.

Cockburn points out the discrepancy between the overwhelming public response to the plight of penguins during the Dassen Island oil spill last year and the often hostile attitude to street children. "The knee-jerk response is to just chase them out of the business district. It's not a solution. We have to face up to the fact that we are a developing country. But all too often it's simply a case of out of sight, out of mind."

After leaving The Homestead I went to a bookshop in Long Street. A middle-aged white man came in to hand out a leaflet. "We represent the victims of human rights abuses," he said. Aha, a defender of the homeless and street children? "We want to make this a crime-free area," he continued. "Our aim is to move on the vagrants, the illegal immigrants and street children." The leaflet says the organisation, "an area response elite", is not a militia or a vigilante group, but "will, however, do whatever is required".

The mother of the young Zimbabwean boy involved in the sjambok incident was more philosophical about it than her white friend. She is an attractive, humorous, successful professional with a PhD and roars with laughter as she recounts the petty humiliations she has to cope with in Cape Town. "I can laugh about these things because I wasn't brought up here, and I can't be angry because that is part of the damage in South Africa," she says. "In my experience Cape Town is worse than the other big cities; it's years behind. Most of my black friends feel the same. Sometimes Cape Town doesn't even feel part of South Africa, and doesn't seem able to cope with the fact that things have moved on and this is Africa.

"I go into a smart shop, for example, to buy something and the assistant will look at me and ask: 'Do you know how much this costs?' They assume that because I'm black, I live in Khayelitsha. Or I go to buy some nice bread in a supermarket and the assistant tells me that the cheap bread is over there. This doesn't happen to me in Johannesburg."

Her son attends one of Cape Town's top schools. "A real little gentleman," she laughs proudly. "But at school a while ago I was told he made up stories about me — do you know, they said, he actually told us his mum was an engineer!" She shrugs. "I had to say, 'Actually, I am.' People here live in such separate worlds. Often whites simply don't know how to talk to you. I turned up for an important meeting at a company and the receptionist wouldn't let me in. She couldn't believe a black person would be participating at a board meeting.

"The coloureds can be the most openly racist. People of all races are so damaged in South Africa. But, you know, I've now had enough of the problems in Cape Town. Social attitudes are often 50 years behind the times! I'm transferring to Jo'burg."

At the GS Jooste hospital in Manenberg, a coloured ghetto and one of the most gang-ridden areas in the Cape Flats, Dr Eula Mothibi fights a daily battle. With scarce resources she has to treat the victims of endemic violence — gunshot and stab wounds — and fight the seemingly unstoppable tides of TB and HIV/Aids. "It is a nightmare; all the time we are sending people home too soon just to make another bed free," she says.

"Most of my white colleagues across town have no idea of these conditions. Here you really see the poverty and you become acutely aware of the huge disparity of wealth in Cape Town."

The bleak, underfunded wards are packed with chronically ill and dying patients. "I come from a township," says Mothibi. "But this disparity angers me. Sometimes you wonder what has changed. Well, the health system has certainly improved in terms of access and people are more aware of their rights — but all most whites say is: things are getting worse. White doctors, who often have very little idea of this huge disparity in services, will be the first to say that. In fact, they're looking for things to go wrong."

Mothibi crisply but unflappably copes with the scenes of misery around her. So it comes as a surprise when she responds, after a long pause, to a query about her feelings regarding the attitudes of the city's white people: "I feel ... anger. In Cape Town you can live very nicely without worrying about anything. Most whites do. All the time I hear people saying that white people here haven't changed."

All the black professionals I spoke to said socially Cape Town is in a dreamlike time warp, but they experience the most direct racism from coloureds. A former underground activist, now married to a coloured woman, said: "I live in a coloured area and my neighbours often make loud, racially derogatory remarks."

Most of us in the Cape live in our racially separate, mutually exclusive worlds. My friend who returned to the Cape from Gauteng is particularly scathing about the smug insularity: "Whites are always saying Cape Town is so laid back — this in a city where gangsterism rules, where rape is endemic and where every type of drug is freely available! Or they purr: 'Cape Town is so much more refined than the rest of the country.'"

History, however, has its own way of reappropriating reality. For example, years after the statue of Van Riebeeck was erected at the bottom of Adderley Street a group called "Afrikaners, Gardens" added a bronze plaque with the following grand legend: "In memory of Jan and Maria van Riebeeck, who brought Christianity and Western Civilisation to South Africa, the country's two most important assets."

This bombastic claim, with all its pompous delusion and racial arrogance, was simply political propaganda. Van Riebeeck did not come to the Cape to gift anything to this country, let alone civilisation; he came to found a provisioning way-station en route to the East and he couldn't wait to escape from what he regarded as a dismal backwater. Ironically, the plaque's shameless fib has been rectified. Recently I noticed it was missing: stolen for its scrap metal value.

The Cape has a long history of separatist dreams: Van Riebeeck planted a bitter almond hedge; Simon van der Stel planned a canal across the Cape Flats, a proposal revived in the 1950s. The idea was to create an island, the Victorian novelist Anthony Trollope remarked approvingly after his visit here in 1877: "Leaving the rest of Africa to its savagery." Even now you still meet influential people who talk wistfully in this vein.

Today Cape Town remains a semi-detached city. To maintain this illusion, however, the Mother City must present an increasingly deceptive cosmetic facade in a hopeless attempt to keep time — and Africa — at bay, like a proud but jaded old trollop.

July 20 2001

A city confused about its parentage

Mike Nicol

It was the headline over Bryan Rostron's insights into Cape Town that rankled. "The last outpost" was such a superficial and outdated way of describing a city in trauma. It offered no empathy with those facing up to that most difficult of all concepts: hybridity. It was dismissive: Cape Town's just a jaded old trollop in a time warp tarted up for the tourists.

As Rostron found, this is true if you see the city as a colonial redoubt busy "sweeping away African realities". My Cape Town is younger and more vital, a teenager: beautiful, caring, dreamy, craving attention, frequently drugged or drunk, liable to be raped, stabbed, shot, cavalier towards HIV and tuberculosis, often angry, given to bombs, fires and in-your-face racism. My city is emerging from a difficult childhood with hard-nosed characteristics but no sense of identity.

This lack of identity is the reason Rostron finds individuals who talk about "pockets of people all living in their own little worlds". In a sense they're right because without a unifying myth Cape Town appears to be a nowhere city, neither part of Africa nor part of Europe. Unfortunately this is the nature of a hybrid city where there is no single story to give everyone a warm glow.

At the moment of Cape Town's founding there were two stories — one told by the Khoi who were dispossessed of their pasturage, the other told by Dutch settlers who founded a way-station on a long trade route. Within seven years a third story was layered on to these when the Dutch East India Company started bringing in slaves, until by 1717 there were more slaves than settlers.

How each group saw Cape Town must have differed markedly: to the slaves a place of suffering; to the Dutch officials a temporary posting; to the settlers a new home; to the Khoi a lost home. With this complexity built into the early city and exacerbated by a change of colonial power when the British took over in 1795, it is no wonder that the "teenage" Cape Town is confused about its parentage.

But the complexity doesn't end there: weaving through these stories is another one about the intimate relationship between the masters and the slaves. As this relationship lasted 180 years — for longer than Cape Town's been a free city — the strength of the bond is considerable. For instance, in many domestic situations master and slave shared house, bed and body. They hated one another; they loved one another. They were interdependent. On the other hand those slaves owned by the company lived by the vagaries of institutional power. Bred in this early history is all Cape Town's current insecurity.

Cape Town is a port. Over the centuries it has had to take in immigrants and refugees. Almost always these groups were not welcomed, in fact were often resented, but were never turned away. Eventually they were accepted and have subsequently added their stories to the city's anthology. If there is anything to be learned here it is that while Cape Town does not exclude foreigners, it does not bother to include them either. New arrivals have to find their own way into the city.

It is this ingrained ambivalence towards newcomers that the recent black immigrants are encountering, and that Rostron reported. Cape Town has always had a black community and, from the first removal in 1910, has tried to keep that community at arm's length. In a loose sense this was part of an unspoken deal between the descendants of the slave masters — whites — and the descendants of the slaves — coloureds — to keep the Cape for themselves. During the days of apartheid there was even a name for it: the Coloured Labour Preference Policy.

That unspoken deal still operates and it is why those blacks who started immigrating to the city with the collapse of such laws as Influx Control in the 1980s feel they're not part of the city. Feel that they're up against blatant racism.

The trouble with Cape Town, a black businessman told me recently, is that while the city has seduced his family, he faces bureaucratic obstacles that prevent him from earning a living here. So he is thinking of moving his business to Johannesburg and commuting. He described his frustration as "climbing a staircase where on every stair people are trying to drag me back and on every landing they are trying to push me down. In Johannesburg I feel I'm on an escalator with people reaching out to help me up."

He believes that he is battling a white and coloured conspiracy. Up to a point he's right; there is a tacit conspiracy. I've heard the coloured voice declare off the record: this is our city, what do blacks want here? What is needed now are coloured voices to articulate publicly the deeper issues behind these sentiments. Until this happens the city will continue to be misunderstood. In the meantime the anguish of a people whose forebears were forcibly brought here to slavery without any chance of going home must be remembered.

This is partly why Cape Town is a city in trauma. The other reason is more obvious if the city's emotional health is measured by the extraordinary levels of violence, and its physical health is measured by the high incidence of tuberculosis and the rising rate of HIV infections. These are the symptoms of a city at odds with itself and its history. Learning to live with many truths and many stories is difficult, and as Cape Town changes under the biggest immigration it has experienced perhaps the trauma should rather be seen as a rite of passage than as a last-ditch attempt by a jaded old trollop to keep Africa at bay.

August 3 2001

NOTES & QUERIES

How can I bring down the forces of global capitalism without losing my well-paid job?
● Firstly wear your cap the right way round; you have to think for yourself; you must be responsible, hard-working, take risks, and so on. To achieve these qualities you have to be a capitalist. You don't need these qualities to wear your cap facing backwards and dance down the street. — *Pete, KwaZulu-Natal*
● 1. Give wildly untruthful answers to market researchers. 2. Never give to the poor and needy: it only saps their will to riot. 3. Indulge in any pointless behaviour that might be deemed irrational by the global capitalist. 4. Deliberately frustrate any desires that may be the result of an advertising campaign. — *Will Davies, London*

Playing out the Crusoe myth

John Matshikiza

In the rosy light of the dawn, a tall black man who carries himself with the coiled grace of a matador is mowing the beach. Well, I don't know if mowing is the right word. The crude machine he is dragging back and forth across the sand in front of the sleeping hotel has no wheels, but the black man is dragging its rough metal barrel, punched with holes at strategic intervals, by a long handle in an action identical to that of the black men who lug mechanical mowers across the impeccable lawns of Sydenham and Rivonia.

The purpose is identical: to hammer a few square metres of Africa back into order for another 24 hours. It is what they call "the end of the small hours" on Africa's Atlantic coast. In a little while the tourists who have come here for a brief respite from the pollution and chaos of the capital city, or who have flown in from the deeper pollution of continents further afield, will be emerging, unashamed of their nakedness for these few days of recreation, sprawling across the beach beneath the blazing sun.

The black man with the easy grace of a matador and the handsome features of a movie star is employed to mow the beach into an image of undisturbed perfection, smoothing away the marks of the previous day's excesses, the tracks of joggers and volleyball players and lovers rolling in the yellow sand. The man is scraping the beach into a manicured evenness that it will lose as soon as the first visitor emerges, blinking the sleep out of crumpled eye-sockets, staggering blindly on to the virgin beach and getting ready for yet another day in paradise.

I have decided that the mowing matador's name is Amadou. Amadou and I are reinforcing the myth created in the yarn of the shipwrecked Robinson Crusoe. Crusoe, or rather his creator, Daniel Defoe, hypnotised us with the idea that there could be a beach, somewhere at the end of the world, that was disturbed by no footsteps other than one's own. One day Crusoe's idyll was shattered when a new set of footsteps appeared before him on the surface of his private planet. At the end of this impertinent trail, when he followed it to its logical conclusion, Crusoe discovered a naked black man. He gave him the unlikely name of "Friday" (because he found him on a Friday) and rapidly introduced him to the concept of domestic service.

I could just have well called my man "Tuesday", since it is on a Tuesday that we surprise each other on this deserted beach. But "Amadou" is the private, unspoken identity that I have chosen to give him instead — an identity appropriate to the real world, rather than this unreal world in which we meet. Amadou and I are almost alone on this privatised stretch of paradise. The sun is still low on the horizon, the sky hanging grey and hazy over the sea. The only other human presence is the silent, uniformed security guard who is eyeing us both, defending this abstract strip of real estate that looks out across the ocean.

Amadou and I do not exchange many words — a brief greeting, and then he is back to his allotted task, working against the tyranny of the clock to make the beach look unreal. He is not paid to ask himself why. I want to stop and take a close look at the mechanics of the machine that he is dragging so carefully back and forth, making sure to keep the lines unnaturally straight in the shifting sands. There is not much to see. The machine has no moving parts. Its only purpose is to make patterns on the sand.

There is not much for Amadou and me to talk about. But we are strangely conspiratorial in the way we refuse to exchange any words about this world that for the moment is inhabited by us alone. Amadou scrapes away in silence, his head down. I make a detour round the patch of beach that he has re-virginised. I choose to let the cuffs of my trousers be soaked by the lapping waves rather than walk defiantly through the sand he has been working so hard to prepare. Together, we tacitly allow others to play out the Robinson Crusoe myth.

But whose beach is this, anyway? Why are we still playing by the rules of a bygone age? After all these years of blood and debate, to whom does Africa belong? I walk far down the beach, till Amadou and his infernal machine, and the first of the sun-blasted tourists drifting on to the beach, are far behind me. It has taken the sun an hour to rise almost halfway to its zenith, baking everything in its path.

There is a fishing village up ahead. On the beach, a knot of black bodies, lightly wrapped in a cacophony of bright colours, is gathered excitedly around a long line of fish netting writhing on the hot sands. The fishermen, a muscular, elite group at the centre of the crowd, are bent low over their nets, working systematically upwards, opening the folds and picking through the living harvest of the sea, separating the valuable queen-sized prawns, the ink-spitting squid and the flat, brainless sole from the mass of small fry. The crowd, the wretched of the Earth, are casually allowed to gather up whatever is left behind.

By tonight the prawns and the calamari will be elaborately laid out on the plates of the tourists at the luxury hotels, at prices that the fishermen could scarcely conceive of in their wildest dreams. The beach will be a dark maze of contradictory human footprints. The sun will be long gone, awaiting its moment to edge over the horizon once more and reveal the lonely figure of Amadou and his mowing machine, preparing the beach for another day in paradise.

August 11 2000

Our new white elephant

Stephen Ellis

The white elephant is a potato. It is a variety that can grow to enormous size but is not good to eat. Amateur gardeners sometimes used to grow white elephant potatoes so they could win first prize at competitions by presenting these impressive-looking but useless lumps of starch. Hence, the description of any misguided prestige project as a "white elephant". Africa has quite a few of them: hospitals, motorways, power stations, built at taxpayers' expense to put money in the pockets of building contractors and their government partners. Nobody bothers much whether they will actually work.

Africa now has a new white elephant. It is called the African Union. Announced as a replacement for the discredited Organisation of African Unity, it promises to become another of the dozens of regional or continental groupings that over the past 40 years have been announced with a flourish but failed to achieve their aims. Some African countries have been members of several such groupings simultaneously, even when these more or less contradict each other in their official aims. If there's a club, join it. It can't do any harm and maybe some funding will come from somewhere. And it looks like evidence of serious planning. That, at least, has been the apparent reasoning of many governments.

Regional cooperation or integration schemes in Africa have generally been set up with either economic or political objectives. Most African governments understandably want to encourage trade with each other rather than with their former colonial metropoles or with the industrialised world. Many also believe that if they can act in a more integrated way they will develop a more powerful political punch. And if the Europeans can do it with their European Union, why can't the Africans do the same? The EU, for all its faults, represents a remarkable development for a continent whose constituent powers were formed by hundreds of years of fighting each other.

The EU did not emerge from ringing declarations of intent only. It was built from the bottom upwards, starting in the 1950s with an agreement on nothing more glamorous than coal and steel. Although it has never been the object of real public affection, it has received an enormous boost from the fact that Europeans travel so much. Many of them visit neighbouring countries for holidays or on business and have learned to appreciate some of the good things they have to offer. This gives the politicians and planners some sort of base in public opinion.

There have been so many failed attempts at African regional cooperation that, rather than starting with a comparison with Europe, it would be better to ask what has gone wrong with previous schemes. With few exceptions, the simple answer is a lack of political will. One project after another has been launched amid noble declarations of solidarity, followed by agreement on reducing tariff barriers and suchlike. Time after time these decisions have not been implemented.

A lack of administrative capacity is part of the reason, but above all it is because the same politicians who will sign up to almost any regional cooperation scheme are scared of the loss of sovereignty that is entailed in putting these ideas into action. All over Africa sovereignty creates jobs and political constituencies that keep politicians in power. Trade with industrialised countries is also at the heart of powerful political lobbies, which create additional reasons for politicians not to boost regional trade.

A close look at African foreign policies confirms the picture. Although they are not devoid of idealism, they are often based on a hard-headed concern to take control of international trade at their neighbours' expense, rather like rival businesses competing for market share. Hence the West African wars, which are partly about who gets control of the region's diamonds, or the partition of the Democratic Republic of Congo by neighbouring countries with an eye on its mineral resources. Outside the pockets of industry (in which South Africa is the leader), African countries have largely mercantile economies in which getting control of trade can only be done at someone else's expense.

Europe was like this in the days of piracy, when the English, Portuguese, Dutch and French would raid each other's ships in struggles for national commercial supremacy. It was in the process of doing this that they established settlements such as Cape Town, which were to be the seeds of later colonies.

Modern industrial economies, which thrive on endlessly expanding consumer markets and continuous increases in productive efficiency, operate differently. They require a different political environment in which international cooperation becomes not only possible but even necessary. This carries its own problems, to be sure. In the very different economies of Africa, grand cooperation projects, designed at the top with little preparation of public opinion, are almost guaranteed to fail. They score high with supporters of pan-African unity and aid donors, and this can make them attractive at first glance. The new African Union promises to be of this type, since it has been prepared with little public debate and in pursuit of grandiose schemes of unity championed by the governments of Libya and Nigeria.

No one doubts Africa's need for a diplomatic forum where governments can consult. Most countries find something like this useful. For that matter, NGOs may find it useful to consult on a continental basis as well. But such an organisation would be far more effective if it could be divorced from the populist but unworkable plans for unity that have brought such disrepute to schemes of this type.

Africa's most pressing need is not for schemes of pan-African unity. It is for real sharing of power between the governors and the governed.

July 26 2001

Get ready, Australia, for another batch

Thebe Mabanga

I am at the Il Pavignione seminar room on the 10th floor of the Michelangelo hotel at Johannesburg's property hotbed, Sandton. Excuse me for stating the obvious, but this place drips with opulence. Not just the credit-fuelled kind found a few floors below us at the Sandton City shopping mall, where the country's upper-middle-class and overnight celebrities display an insatiable urge to live beyond their means. Up here the seriously wealthy have gathered to examine investment and immigration opportunities in Australia.

They are at ease with their affluence and conscience; they are pricey without being too ostentatious and instinctively cagey. The seminar room we are in can squeeze in 100 people. This evening, about 80 seats have been made available to allow for breathing space. Upon registration the gentleman in attendance, Erick, recognises me from my call to book a place. It is probably because I am the youngest or maybe because I am one of two black people attending. Either way, I stand out.

The audience just about fills the room. It is an interesting mix of the old and the new upper class. There are many white couples. The men look like they are at the peak of their careers. There are also a few white men who appear to be at the autumn of a life of luxury built on inheritance and the benefits of apartheid, clearly attending to prepare for retirement in Oz. Then there is a breed that looks set to define the new face of the super rich: young Indian males. The few who have made it tonight are either with partners or in small groups. In my row are two who look too young to afford property in Australia and too hip to consider living among kangaroos in the excessively pale, sometimes uninspiring colonial outpost down under.

The presenter of the seminar, Margaret Jurca, is a very interesting proposition. Her accent suggests she is an East European native and she later tells us she has lived in Australia since 1969. She has made a name for herself as an international property consultant over the past 16 years. She comes with a prime recommendation as the Wespac Businesswoman of the year for 2000. She has impeccable credentials and has been coming to South Africa for the past four years. How interesting.

When I speak to people in academic and business circles they tell me how difficult it is — thanks to the Department of Home Affairs — to get skilled people into South Africa. Yet here is a woman, with virtually a free pass into the country (the last time she was here was six weeks ago), whose sole mission is to entice our wealthiest and, debatably, most talented individuals away. She does so with what would be smooth talking were it not for her accent and zeal.

One thing she did was to crush my view that Australia is uninspiring. The first half of a 75-minute session was dedicated to investment opportunities, and her place of choice is the Gold Coast in North Eastern Australia. From an economic perspective the place is a gem: it is hardly the size of Johannesburg but has A$20-billion investment committed to it. It has just witnessed the opening of the $5 000-a-night Versace hotel. It has an eight-lane, $750-million highway linking it to Brisbane and in 2005 it will be the world golfing capital, with 71 golf courses.

Yet for all this apparent lustre, the audience is impressed but not inquisitive, thus preventing me from asking the question I had all evening: Do they need semi-cheap labour? Gardener, dishwasher, caddie? Anything.

The second half of the session on migrating proves livelier. Jurca starts by noting: "It is easy to adjust to life in Australia because we drive on the same side of the road, we speak the same language [since when?]." But hang on, I've heard this one before. Oh, I eavesdropped on Jurca reciting the mantra to the hip Indians. She then gives us what sounds like a history lesson from 2030: "When South Africans first migrated to Australia, they settled in Perth [on the West Coast]. Then they realised that it is isolated and then they made their way inland."

The questions flow thick and fast, with one old man inquiring with exasperation: "When can I move in?" What I can say is that South Africans primed for emigration — or those preparing a landing pad by investing abroad — appear to have grown more diplomatic in explaining their plans. "South Africa's a beautiful country, it's got great potential, but just look at the Aids thing," was one offering. Get ready, Australia, for another batch.

October 27 2000

The lost white tribe down under

Matthew Krouse

P erth: the city white South African dreams are made of. Nestling serenely on the banks of the mighty Swan river (more a coastal estuary) it fits contradictory descriptions. If one goes there one hears them all. One Australian calls Perth "a shopping mall with a river running through it". A South African who's settled there in enviable comfort calls the place "Bloemfontein with skyscrapers".

On the plane, just before landing, one gets a whiff of the mixture of pride and paranoia that characterises the denizens of down under. A list is circulated of illegal substances that may not be brought into Australia — a country boasting low levels of disease. A video is shown on the airplane's movie screen depicting a sniffer dog, its nose buried in suitcases, being led around the busy baggage receiving hall of Perth airport by a sexy Camel Man of a cop. The creature can apparently detect 30 forbidden things, from drugs to exotic wooden crafts.

In the video an elderly Chinese woman confesses that in her luggage she's stashed some vacuum-packed sausages from home. The Camel Man confiscates these with a stern nod and she's hit with a steep fine. But, travellers are told, there are bins before customs sporting big signs in which the bad stuff may be dumped. Official-looking pamphlets tell lascivious Australians that, if it's discovered they've had sex with children on their sojourns, they can expect the worst.

These are clues to what one suspects is an inner fear of white Australians who find themselves on the verge of the mighty Asian tiger — a fear of being swamped by Eastern cultures far more indigenous and rooted to the region than their own. Everywhere one goes one sees Asian immigrants eking out a meagre living from the great Australian dream. As an outsider it's difficult to surmise who these people really are, but one can see from the place they occupy in the urban food chain that they are a lesser merchant class battling like hell to stay afloat.

But this isn't the case with Perth's expatriate white South Africans. They, in contrast, are leading a full and prosperous life on the opposite end of the Indian Ocean, far from the messy democratisation still taking place back home. They're visible in the distinctly local things they've chosen to lug with them. In Perth one finds branches of Nando's takeaway chicken, 11 Bothas are listed in the telephone book, there's a South Africa Club and a Jewish school attended by lots of South African kids.

After years of seeping immigration, Australians now know their South African neighbours well. A well-worn phrase gets repeated in a broad Australian accent, attempting to mimic ours: "Thu cors in thu groj." It translates with comforting sanity. Yes, for South Africans who've settled there, the car's sure to be tucked away safely, in the garage.

It's in this sunny, litterless scape that the city holds its showcase Perth International Arts Festival, in conjunction with the University of Western Australia. The fact that it runs on government funds seems to keep everyone yakking about how money for culture should be responsibly spent. Broad-based public concern for the arts is so un-South African: we leave decisions about what we're going to see to corporate sponsors who make a big noise when it comes to self-promotion. In Australia one seldom sees the type of corporate branding of the arts that one sees here. It's considered vulgar.

Perth's headline act this year is a short season of dance by the ever-challenging choreographer Merce Cunningham, who established himself as an über-guru back in the Fifties in collaboration with composer John Cage. On February 3 the city's upper crust arrived in full force at the enormous Burswood auditorium to see Cunningham's company do a retrospective of works designed by pop art idols Andy Warhol and Robert Rauschenberg. In the thousand-odd seater venue situated alongside a casino, not unlike Caesar's in Kempton Park, I sat between a former South

African dance teacher, who took notes throughout the performance, and a well-preserved, elderly South African dentist and his overdressed Australian wife.

The atmosphere was cordial and, to use a modern South African insult, Eurocentric. But still, Perth just doesn't feel First World. Its opening nights are full of pretentious hugs and kisses — a very intimate culture club: everybody seems to know everybody else. It felt like a night at Pretoria's State Theatre back in 1974.

But Western Australia is branching out at a rate that puts us to shame, becoming more inclusive of all the types they encounter in their regular lives. That's why I was there in the first place. Australians are going all out to hold a dialogue with what they term the Indian and Pacific rims. One wonders why. They really have everything at their disposal. There's only one problem, though: they feel terribly isolated in what one Aussie called "the arsehole end of the world".

Feeling far apart has led them to go out and find what it is they think they want to see. The office of the Perth Festival, for example, sent its performing arts manager, Sally Sussman, shopping for plays to our National Arts Festival in Grahamstown last year. Before departing Sussman did a little research and came up with a fascinating fact about past Australian-South Africa cultural relations: "In the Fifties there was an Indian Ocean rim festival connecting many countries from the region. It was, I guess, more a community festival and they went to incredible lengths to get people out here. I think it folded in the Seventies."

It didn't take Sussman much effort to discover a willing audience base — the big South African community in Perth. To make tangible links she contacted what she calls "a virtual African studies community, run by someone called Peter Limb". Here she discovered the Grahamstown festival, where she came upon suitable practitioners, like the crazy theatre director Brett Bailey, who was planning a new work about Idi Amin. Sadly, the play wasn't ready for Perth this year.

Sussman also saw the internationally famous Handspring Puppet Company's *The Chimp Project*, which turned out to be too expensive for her festival to import. "We needed to start out with a few projects that represent different aspects of South African work, rather than blow all our money on one event," she says. Combing the discount rack Sussman travelled to Durban where, on an out-of-town excursion, she met up with a pantsula jive group from Umlazi called the Durban Township Boys.

I saw the Umlazi boys do two outdoor performances in the public gathering places of Perth. On February 8 they did a frantic little show in a constricted space between two rows of benches in front of an information kiosk in the city busport. They didn't exactly crack it. Their backing tape was too loud and the space was too small for them to move with any ease. It was their first performance and they were probably missing the wild abandon of the African street on a busy day.

They had my sympathies. The Australian commuters, bustling by on the way to their buses, didn't quite know what to make of these black youths in their tracksuits roaring into their mics. Some stood by watching for a couple of minutes wearing those fixed grins whites tend to break into when the blacks start doing something culturally exclusive in a language they can't understand. It's funny how universal these things are.

I caught the Umlazi boys once again, by mistake. I was crossing an outdoor piazza two days later when I heard the familiar strains of kwaito wafting through the air. I hurried over to where the performance was happening and there was the troupe with a grand audience now, much more relaxed. There were also new additions to their crew: four doting white teenage Aussie girls, each one clutching the tracksuit top of her African holiday romance while the boys danced in the sun.

Perth and Durban are basically trying hard to fall in love. Cultural planners of both port cities are using the fact that the two share the same latitude and ocean to indicate something deep and meaningful that will help forge their bonds. One gets the feeling, though, that what they do have in common, more than geography, is a low sense of self-esteem. Both cities are regarded as being of minor cultural significance to their countries.

The romance was sealed last year when Durban mayor Obed Mlaba flew over to open an exhibition of African wire and metal craft that showed in Fremantle, a trendy coastal spot outside Perth. This was preceded by a cross-cultural exchange project between the fine art umbrella body, the Artists Foundation of Western Australia, and Durban's Bat Centre. KwaZulu-Natal craft workers — beadworker Ntombifuti Magwasa, model car maker Michael Mbatha and telephone wire basket maker Vincent Sithole — demonstrated their skills in Perth, and renowned Australian textile artist Nalda Searles came to the Bat Centre.

The South African crafts shown in Perth sold well. Planner Jenny Wright of the Artists Foundation found the African craft had "a broader audience than a lot of cutting-edge contemporary art. I'm sometimes a little suspicious of the 'look at the cute ethnic' craft aspect to it," she says. "Perhaps I shouldn't disparage that because there's tremendous interest and people wanted to buy. They hadn't seen work like that before."

Wright hints at the culture shock experienced by the African artists on their journey into the big wide world — language barriers, etcetera. But that was last year's Perth festival. This year, in addition to the Umlazi boys, the programme showcased two South African plays. Heinrich Reisenhoffer's and Oscar Petersen's *Suip*, a hit last year at Grahamstown, must have confirmed a planeload of ex-South African fears. Upon arrival at the Octagon Theatre, at the University of Western Australia, one was confronted by prominently displayed warnings that the language would be bad, but it would be in Afrikaans. In case anyone couldn't understand the bad language there was a glossary on page one of the programme listing foul words like *poes, naai, kont* and the well-worn phrase *jou ma se ...*

Suip is 90% in Afrikaans. It's a frightening work, masterfully acted by what appear to be genuine bergies trying to fathom how, in history, they've gotten to be who they are. Of course it's all put didactically down to drink. The auditorium was brimming with South Africans who must have been thanking the Lord that they and their money were now safely on the other side. *Suip* does not say to our lost brethren, "Please come home."

There were Australian-South Africans of all hues. Posh Lenasia Indians sat alongside Africans who looked like they belonged to our diplomatic corps. Meanwhile, their teenage kids looked and spoke like Aussies. The play was so in-your-face that the mirth eventually turned to stress. So when the really funny moments popped up the laughter seemed a little too forced. There was a South African Indian who was having such a homegrown cultural experience that his eyes were watering and he was virtually rolling in the aisle. After interval I noticed that a smart, severe-looking, coloured Capetonian woman beside me had not returned.

On February 9, at sunset in the campus gardens, Ellis Pearson and Bheki Mkhwane did their kiddies show, *A Boy Called Rubbish*. It was yet another full house of nostalgic South Africans who, at this stage, I was beginning to suspect may actually consider themselves driven into exile against their will. From what I saw I can safely say I don't think much of Pearson's and Mkhwane's work. The two seem to think they're the funniest things on earth when, actually, there's very little humour in what they do. Their act is all over the place and their props, which they boast can all be found on a trash heap, are not that skilfully used. And their supposed tale of endurance, of a boy who saves his village, is virtually impossible to understand.

The audience in the sunken garden of the university, though, had a very good South African time. Across the way from me there was a young Afrikaans couple cosily nestled on a blanket with their baby. They were drinking a litchi Liquifruit and chewing biltong. The hot sun was setting, and my disorientation was beginning to set in.

The next day I found more evidence of South African artistry, this time in the Art Gallery of Western Australia. A glossy catalogue produced by the gallery and sold at their bookshop shows that, for last year's festival, they brought in the work of three major South African artists in a collaboration called *Home*. The process of procuring works for the exhibition began in 1997 when the gallery's curator of contemporary art, Trevor Smith, visited Cape Town and Johannesburg to source material that would appear alongside artists from Canada, Eastern Europe, North Africa and the United States.

The three artists Smith selected were David Goldblatt, Zwelethu Mthethwa and Kendell Geers. Mthethwa's photographs are colourful portraits of township life; Goldblatt went strolling with his camera on a special assignment to some asbestos mines in the Australian outback settlement of Wittenoom. Geers went out on the attack, taking his installation on to the city streets where he put up his work called *48 Hours* in bus stops around Perth.

Basically, Geers's work is a series of backlit inkjet pieces of text that really shine out at night. Where adverts would normally be placed in the bus stops, Geers's work names shocking crimes that, one assumes, took place in Gauteng in the late Nineties. Here's a taste: "Six gunmen opened fire on the drinking occupants of a shack ...", "Constable MS Lamola of Ennerdale police station was mugged ..." and "a bank robber was shot dead ...".

Expatriate South Africans must have shuddered each time they drove past, receiving further confirmation that the country is now beyond repair. Isn't it amazing how the art of someone like Geers can appear so reactionary once it's removed from its context? I had seen the work previously on the outside walls of the newly established Camouflage gallery in Johannesburg where it made a very weak statement, reiterating facts South Africans already knew.

But here's a quote from the *Home* catalogue, written by Smith, the show's curator, that can be used in defence of Geers's idea. "Of course Perth's crime rate is nowhere near that of Johannesburg," Smith writes. "Indeed it has been something of a safe haven for many wealthy, mostly white, South Africans seeking refuge from the crime and violence of Johannesburg. Yet like most cities Perth has its own particular brand of urban paranoia bred by its nearly empty night-time streets. If fear eats the soul (to borrow from Fassbinder), sitting at a lonely bus stop reading litanies of anonymous death may not be so good for your health. On the surface we may count our blessings, but under the skin we are not so confident."

So what is the basis of this lack of confidence? Perhaps it can be found in the truth of Australia's own shady past. They're hardly free of race politics. They've also managed quite successfully to fence off Aboriginal culture, subtly relegating it to a space where, for white audiences, it can be viewed in safety. Aboriginal artists themselves, it is claimed, support the fact that the Art Gallery of Western Australia has a hall reserved especially for their art. Because specific commercial galleries sell Aboriginal painting only they tend to appear just a rung above the curio chain called Creative Native. It is a form of representation that, in South Africa, we have seen come and go.

The small Aboriginal community of Perth is serviced by a single nine-year-old theatre company called Yirra Yaakin Noongar Theatre, meaning "stand tall". Run as an incorporated association, members have to have Aboriginal origins in order to have voting rights. They vote in a board that runs the company on behalf of the local community.

Two CEOs run the show — Paul MacPhail, who takes care of the admin, and David Milroy, who looks into the art. The company owns a minibus and employs eight office staff, who work in an old government function centre in town. A portion of their funding comes from grants received from the state funding body, Arts WA, the rest from ticket sales. Yirra Yaakin Noongar's freelance Aboriginal performers do about three major productions in Perth's professional theatres each year. They tour their work nationally and this year they will be developing their own humble venue into a functioning playhouse.

At this year's festival they put on a one-woman show called *Alice*, the rambling testimony of a young woman of colour whose life has had far more downs than ups. Spiced up with some gritty live rock, it's the true story of its author and performer, Alice Haines, who has seen family violence, poverty and a small degree of hometown fame.

It is a poignant work, evoking a tired response from its middle-upper-class, suburban audience: "We've heard it all before." Alice's pathetic life story, like so many, seems dwarfed by major First World cultural interventions that come to Perth in its festival season. Audience members probably regard their tax contribution better spent on cultural highs such as the Royal Shakespeare Company's production of Carlo Goldini's *A Servant to Two Masters,* songs by Mahler performed by the West Australian symphony and video art by world-class artists Bill Viola and Stan Douglas.

In comparison to these internationally regarded events, South Africa's cultural contribution also seemed meagre. But the dialogue is happening, not necessarily because Australians have now met up with South Africans who've packed for Perth. Indeed, there's a healthier curiosity about South Africans who've decided, for whatever reason, to stay home.

February 23 2001

Streetgate torpedoes the opposition

Mungo Soggot

It was the telephone call from Johan Smit which drummed home that the petition fraud was a vintage National Party exercise. A few hours before the *Mail & Guardian* went to press with what would become known as "streetgate", Smit telephoned a reporter in the Cape Town office to find out what the paper was up to in Manenberg, one of the Mother City's most treacherous townships.

The paper had been asking Manenberg residents how or if they were approached by National Party representatives to express their opinion on mayor Peter Marais's street renaming plan. One resident — probably a party organiser — had alerted Smit, a mayoral henchman, to the newspaper's investigation. The alacrity with which National Party command back in Cape Town was briefed signalled that the party's famously efficient management of the Cape Flats electorate was in full swing.

It was not a good day for Smit. That afternoon, when approached for comment, he effectively accused the newspaper of stealing the petitions from the council. When he got nowhere with this, he suggested the paper had forged the petitions.

A few public inquiries and several months later, the gist of the M&G's investigation was confirmed: Marais's office had presided over a scheme to fraudulently manipulate a sampling of public opinion for the controversial plan to rename Adderley and Wale streets after FW de Klerk and Nelson Mandela. Petitions with forged signatures had been drawn up, as those responsible sought to conjure overwhelming public support for the initiative. The various probes into the scam resulted in the suspension of officials and the death of the street renaming plan.

That was just the beginning. The saga also triggered the expulsion of Marais. And it set in motion a chain of events that broke the Democratic Alliance, after the DP and NNP wrestled publicly over what to do with Marais. The DP had its way in the end, but only after its shaky alliance with the NNP had been irreparably harmed.

By National Party standards, the petition fraud — and the accompanying lies to the public — was small fry: no money was stolen and nobody was hurt. The fraudsters were, in fact, bumbling incompetents. According to a handwriting expert consulted by the *M&G*, they pulled off some of the most pathetic forgeries he had ever witnessed. The object of the fraud — Marais's streetnaming plan — merely highlighted the ebullient mayor's fondness for cashing in on South Africa's past.

Yet despite such inherent triviality, the saga had a major impact, because it exemplified the difference between the DP and the NNP, and therefore provided the first major test of their rocky marriage. John Matisonn of The Sunday Independent captured it best when he said the street naming project revealed the "Boer maak a plan" mentality of the Nats — compared with the prissier and more methodical approach to politics pursued by the DP, which is particularly fond of testing public opinion with real polls. It was fitting that during the final round of the battle between the Nats and the DP over Marais, a secret poll conducted by the DP was leaked. The extensive survey of the Cape electorate revealed, among other things, that Marais was not nearly as popular as the Nats claimed — and, putting the boot in, showed the street renaming exercise was a dud with the voters.

The saga self-evidently showed off the worst of the Nats — opportunism, mendacity and a consistent disregard for the public. It provided ample ammunition for anyone arguing that the DP deserved the worst for getting into bed with the National Party in the first place. By teaming up with the NNP in 2000, the DP gambled against accepting the fact that the future in South Africa is black, and instead opted for the lion's share of the white electorate. If anything would have prompted them to regret their bet, it was Streetgate.

Apart from being severely embarrassed by the Nats' antics, the DP also got the chance to show off its professed commitment to clean government. But it also got the opportunity to demonstrate some questionable judgement itself, most notably where the appointment of Willem Heath to probe the affair was concerned. The DP had championed Heath when, while still in charge of his special investigating unit, he crossed swords with the ANC. Now was their chance to use him, albeit after he had left public service and set up a private consultancy.

There is no doubt Heath's integrity is beyond reproach, and that he has a nose for doing the right thing. With hindsight, though, he was the wrong choice. After a week's hearings, Heath rapidly produced a report blasting Marais and his henchmen, but lacking proof of their guilt.

His report evaluated the evidence from the hearings, including that of Victoria Johnson, the Cape council's legal adviser who spilled the beans on much of the detail surrounding the vote fraud. But Heath's probe did not rely on much investigation. Crucially, it did not establish the chain of command — who had told whom to forge. This made it easier for the NNP to attack the Heath report when the DP sought to use it to justify ousting Marais. The fact that Heath was seen to be an ally of the DP, and especially its leader Tony Leon, made the former judge more vulnerable to the charge he was a hired gun. Leon and Heath were particularly exposed because of the zeal with which Leon had appointed the advocate. The DP leader did so after receiving an affidavit from Johnson, the legal adviser, and — against her wishes — went public with it and called in the corruption buster. Not treatment that is likely to encourage whistleblowers.

Before Johnson appeared, the Democratic Alliance had launched some low-profile inquiries, one of which headed by a Cape senior counsel hand-picked by Ben Kieser, the council's legal chief who was subsequently spit-braaied by Heath for his handling of the saga.

By the end of October, the conflict between the DP and the Nats had exploded, the DP calling for the dissolution of the New National Party. It has been widely said that Streetgate was the excuse the DP needed to flush out Marais — one of the Nats' main weapons — and generally establish its ascendancy over its alliance partners. It has even been suggested that the original story was leaked by the DP — which, without going into any detail, the *M&G* can unequivocally deny. In the end, the saga had too great an effect, destroying the alliance itself.

If the Nats do disappear, the country will be robbed of a particular brand of politician that, at the very least, produces great political drama. Even during the dark days of National Party rule, there was a comic, absurd touch to the party, as was so ably demonstrated by the novelist Tom Sharpe. That tradition was continued during Streetgate, only this time without the savagery of apartheid.

The day after the *M&G's* first exposé, Smit and co were mainly concerned with discovering and punishing the M&G's sources — and then appointing what they hoped was a tame inquiry. Little did they know that the cavalier massaging of public opinion would mean much more trouble than that. It would, in fact, deal a mortal blow to the party that ruled South Africa for much of the 20th century, and torpedo the official opposition.

October 2001

The Mail & Guardian *exposed the street-renaming saga in a series of articles starting on June 8 2001. At the end of October, New National Party leader Marthinus van Schalkwyk announced the withdrawal of the NNP from the Democratic Alliance*

Why the M&G matters

Drew Forrrest

"**W**hy go to that right-wing rag?" was one government official's response when told that I was moving to the *Mail & Guardian*. It was not untypical. There is a quite general perception — not only in ruling circles — that the newspaper has drifted rightwards since its heyday in the late 1980s and that its deep editorial sympathies may even lie with the Democratic Alliance.

The hostility of African National Congress leaders, partly by osmosis from the presidency, has reached bizarre proportions. When the *M&G* asked earlier this year whether President Thabo Mbeki was fit to rule, certain ANC leaders saw it as a significant echo of a speech by DA leader Tony Leon in Parliament days earlier. It is even suggested that editor Howard Barrell holds clandestine strategy meetings with DA leaders.

Presidential communications officers are loath to speak on the record to the *M&G*, and there appears to be a policy in some state departments of refusing to speak to the paper at all. Some ANC politicians have stooped to the practice, virtually unknown in other democracies, of suing the paper.

For anyone who knows Barrell, the DA conspiracy theory is ludicrously false. But the "rightward drift" charge is more plausible. The Democratic Party, and now the DA, has received some surprisingly sympathetic treatment in the *M&G*, particularly before the 1999 election. There is nothing criminal in this — as the official opposition the DA deserves intelligent coverage. But it is not by any stretch of the imagination a party of the left.

Coupled with this is what is construed as the paper's consistently negative portrayal of the ANC government, a "racist" focus on corruption involving black politicans and officials, and a cruelly personal vendetta against Mbeki. Much of the outrage in the ruling party comes from a sense of betrayal — that a newspaper that once, at great risk, agitated for democratic change has now crossed to the enemy. It is curious that genuinely conservative publications like *Die Burger,* which once described the truth commission as "a scorpion under a stone", attract almost no ANC attention.

The *M&G's* perceived shift is largely an optical illusion. At its best, it has combined elements of a serious left-leaning publication like the *New Statesman* and the satirical hell-raiser, *Private Eye*. In its world-view, and the mentality of the journalists who continue to work for it, the *M&G* has changed very little. It has always been an anti-establishment paper, rather than a party mouthpiece, and the leaders of the ANC are undeniably the country's new political establishment. It is this that makes it possible for the paper to carry a softish double-page interview with Leon, while editorialising in lavish praise of the South African Communist Party. Both, in the new South Africa, are political outsiders.

But the fact is that it spares no erring politician or political movement, regardless of where they stand on the spectrum. How does the charge of DA bias square with the *M&G*'s most influential political exposé of the year, on the Peter Marais vote-rigging saga? The story has done serious damage to the unity of the DA in the Western Cape, and perhaps to its electoral prospects in a region it wants to use as a governance showpiece.

The "mainstream" media in South Africa operate for the most part in the same way, but the difference lies in the *M&G*'s tradition of journalistic extremism. It will run stories the mainstream papers will not touch, either because of the risk element or considerations of taste. Democracies need at least one paper of this kind, because it gives the truth a better chance of making it into the open.

The approach has the defects of its qualities. The *M&G* can be spectacularly right, as it was over the shenanigans of former Central Energy Fund chairperson Keith Kunene. But the cult of dauntlessness can also lead to inaccuracy and excess — hence the fact that the *M&G* faces more defamation suits than any other South African publication.

The other root of the paper's unusual brand of risk-taking independence is its owner, *The Guardian*, and the Scott Trust, which insulates publications of the Guardian group from management interference. Assuming *The Guardian* retains a controlling stake for a good few years, the *M&G* may grow in importance as a standard-bearer of intrepid journalism in South Africa.

This is because any threat to media independence is unlikely to come from legislative change or informal repression à la Zimbabwe. It will come more insidiously, through interventionist owners. As the case of Rupert Murdoch makes clear, this is a worldwide problem for the media. Hence the *M&G*'s editorial concerns about overtures to possible partners, including certain black empowerment groups.

These concerns are not racist. The crisp issue is the almost obsessive interest some empowerment bosses have in the media, and their strong links with the ruling party. They are open to political pressures, which they may transmit to editors. But they may be more interested in advancing their own fortunes than those of the ANC, and this is just as much of a threat. An energetic political climber like Nail's Saki Macozoma is unlikely to be a hands-off proprietor. Given the *M&G*'s precarious finances, what is the nature of his interest in the publication?

There is another area where the *M&G* may have a unique contribution to make — as an aid to rebuilding a left-wing project in South Africa. It would not mean indiscriminate opposition to government and the ANC, nor uncritical support for the unions and the SACP. There are left elements in the government's programme, and many ANC members remain true to its proud traditions. By the same token, the labour movement is far from infallible. A case in point was its knee-jerk resistance to the iGoli 2002 plan, designed to lift Johannesburg from bankruptcy.

In a small way, the *M&G* can help define a left agenda in a post-apartheid and post-communist age. Its starting point must be that there are no more simple verities, and nothing can be taken for granted. SACP secretary general Jeremy Cronin used the term "socialism" half a dozen times in a recent article in the *M&G*, without defining it. One assumes he does not mean Tony Blair's "Third Way". But can he possibly mean the fabled worker state, raised on the ruins of private property?

The *M&G* faces its toughest challenge since it started as a semi-*samizdat* news-sheet 16 years ago. The whole newspaper industry is groaning under adverse market conditions, and some well-known publications look close to the brink. The losses the *M&G* sustained last year cannot continue indefinitely. To survive, it must get better. It must bash less, sloganeer less, and explain more. It must hold a more intense focus on the issues of the day.

The government and the ANC must appreciate that it is not a respectable mainstream paper and will lose its *raison d'être* if it tries to become one. It must observe the standard canons of accuracy and fairness, in the sense of getting all versions of the story and giving the right of reply. But it cannot be so fair as to lose its sense of outrage and slide into mealy-mouthed neutrality.

The government's refusal to talk to the paper is silly and self-defeating — it makes no sense to accuse it of bias and then stonewall it when approached for comment or information. It breaches a basic political groundrule: engage your critics. Politicians, like Minister in the Office of the President Essop Pahad, who see the media as an adjunct of the government information service, are probably a lost cause.

But the true democrats in the ANC — and there are many of them, including Cabinet ministers — should be helping the *M&G* get its facts and perspectives straight. They should see the paper as a flattering reflection on, and institution of, South Africa's democracy.

September 7 2001

My tourist war in Afghanistan

Stefaans Brümmer

*"Asia is a living body, and Afghanistan its heart. In the ruin of the heart
lies the ruin of the body. So long as the heart is free, the body remains
free. If not, it becomes a straw adrift in the wind."*
— Mohammed Iqbal (1876-1938)

"Same old shit!" an American voice exploded where I slept on my
bed of dusty concrete corridor. I dragged myself to a higher consciousness and mustered a croaky, "What shit?"

"Lollipop!" the voice boomed back through layers of morning haze and
the layers of sleep I had yet to penetrate. In that instant my week in
Afghanistan made complete sense, which is to say it made no sense at all.

Sense and no sense seemed, at the time, perfect equivalents. I tried to
verbalise that insight and to hang on to it, but the reader will have to
excuse me if I failed and make less sense now. Welcome to Afghanistan,
the land of seamless contradiction, the land where shit and lollipop are
identical twins.

The loud American voice I learned that night belonged to Tom, a giant
of a man and a senior staffer with a large United States television network.
He, like I, was one of perhaps 500 journalists who had made it into
Afghanistan in the weeks that followed September 11. He, unlike I, had
brought with him a dozen or more colleagues and support staff, broadcast
equipment and creature comforts to match and, of course, booze to fill a bar.

That morning, the morning of the booming revelation, was the morning I was to have left Afghanistan. I stumbled from my concrete patch
determined to wash, but again there was no water in the drum that served
50-odd journalists with only a couple of refills a day, carted by a decrepit
little man and his two donkeys. We were holed up in a compound belonging to the "foreign ministry" of the opposition Northern Alliance. The
town was Khwaja-Bahawudin in the north-east, where the alliance main-
tained a military headquarters of sorts about 25km from the front line.

Before 8am I was at the ministry office, asking to leave town and cross
the border back to neighbouring Tajikistan. Zubeir, the official who controlled our every move and dispensed or withheld permissions for reasons
we all failed to fathom, told me to return at 10am. When I did so, he told
me I should have come at nine "like all the others". Catch.

I shall not bore the reader with a rendition of my endeavours the rest of the day, save to say that by nightfall a dozen of us had done enough clamouring for Zubeir to let us go and promise to radio the border guards to let us through. Three cars bumped and grinded into the night; past the "refugee hotel" where earlier I had photographed my little enigma girl; past the place where two more South Africans and I had crossed a river on overpriced horseback to get to the front; past two checkpoints manned by boys with guns.

At a third checkpoint we skidded to a halt a little late and the soldier on duty levelled his rifle first at the windshield; then settled on a front tyre — a rather civilised gesture I thought. But then the soldier and one half of our Siamese driver greeted each other warmly and the tyre was spared.

The late stop appeared to be a function, or rather the dysfunction, of the Siamese driver. It was like this: we understood a jovial man named Shah Mahmood, who sang as he drove, to be the driver of the battered jeep three more journalists and I had piled into that evening. But Shah Mahmood wanted to take a friend and there was no more space. No problem. They shared the drivers' seat, one on the lap of the other. In the darkness we saw a single body with two heads. Whether they shared the controls we could only speculate.

When we reached the Pyandzh river, the border with Tajikistan, talk was of the proximity of beer. Afghanistan is a dry country and few of us had that luxury during our stay. But the beer would have to wait. We waited half an hour, maybe more, for the painstaking process of passport inspection to begin and for the steel ferry, powered by an old tractor mounted on top, to crank into action. The wait was normal and punctuated by shots in the distance, which was also normal. But eventually word came that the Russian troops who controlled the border area on the Tajik side, our next hurdle, had "no programme for the night".

Our consolation was that when we returned to the compound at Khwaja-Bahawudin at around midnight, Tom invited us into the rooms his network had been assigned by the Northern Alliance and promptly issued us with a beer and some shots of vodka each. But the mood was grim. Tom and his colleagues were still up, discussing the news that had just reached them of an anthrax attack on the US network NBC's headquarters in New York — among the first of many anthrax scares. Some of them knew the secretary who had contracted the disease after opening an envelope. They drank, and drank, to her health.

Tom boomed: "I say kill them all." After some argument he toned it down: "Kill 50% or 25%. What would you say is a good place to draw the line?" Eventually he settled on the US colonising Afghanistan. Among the initiatives he suggested was that the tractor ferry at the Pyandzh be replaced with Daffy and Donald Duck boats. Journalists wanting to cross the border could do so in the Disney theme of their choice. I feared Tom's diatribe was more prophetic than he intended.

The next day we got out. Shah Mahmood was a single driver again; the Russians had a programme and the ferry was running; the tank shells that were flying regularly now were exploding beyond the next hill; and on the Tajik side a stoned border guard with a half-deck of golden teeth and the apparent need for more let us pass for the small consideration of $25 each.

At one of the Russian checkpoints that followed we had an interesting conversation. The soldiers claimed their spies inside Afghanistan had just informed them of the whereabouts of Osama bin Laden. And so it is that I can report exclusively to you, the reader, that the most wanted man in the world is holed up near the village of Soboori, not far from the town of Jalalabad in Eastern Afghanistan. Scoop?

It was with scoop — an exclusive — in mind that I had left Johannesburg three weeks earlier, a fortnight after the September 11 attacks on the US. Fool! I had motivated the trip to my editor by saying that the world's media were congregating in Pakistan, clamouring to get into Afghanistan with little chance of success. Unlike they, I would get in, I told him, via the former Soviet republic of Tajikistan where I would link up with the Afghan opposition Northern Alliance and enter the sliver of territory they held. I could be one of a few journalists to reach Afghan soil. At the time that seemed truthful.

Dushanbe is an overgrown one-horse town. It is also the capital of Tajikistan, a country served mainly· by one airline, Tajikistan Airlines, which connects it most days to Moscow and weekly to Istanbul and Munich. Tajikistan Airlines' aircraft are the only I have encountered that are infested with flies (flies catching a flight) and where water drips from the ceilings. But these are not the hardships I want to talk about; rather let me share my grief at seeing my exclusive slip away.

In London, where earlier I picked up my Afghan and Russian visas, an initial drip of media reports from Northern Alliance territory turned into a shower. In Moscow, where a Tajik visa had to be obtained and days spent fighting on to a Tajikistan Airlines flight to Dushanbe, it became a cloudburst. CNN kept screening the same footage of a Northern Alliance tank firing into the distance, accompanied by the latest from "our correspondent in Afghanistan".

And so it should have come as no surprise that when I arrived in Dushanbe, the town was bursting with others like me, a few hundred hopefuls clamouring to join the perhaps 300 who by then had already made it into Afghanistan. I filed a dispatch describing a constant stream of khaki camera jackets "as worn by gung-ho journalists everywhere" tracing a triangular route between the Tajik foreign ministry, the Northern Alliance representative office and the Hotel Tajikistan. The latter was a Soviet-era concrete monstrosity where most of the khaki jackets hung out. The Tajik ministry and the Alliance office were the bureaucratic hurdles the jackets had to negotiate before entry to Afghanistan became theoretically possible.

The next morning I got my first taste of Afghanistan. It clogged the taste buds, gritted the eyes, matted the hair. When later I reported to my editor that I had half the Afghan desert up my nostrils and that various bodily excretions consisted mainly of dust, the exaggeration was within the bounds of poetic license. What had first seemed to be a thick fog that rolled into Dushanbe turned out to be a storm of fine dust from the barren plains of Afghanistan 250km south. The dust severely restricted visibility and the Northern Alliance suspended flights to the patch of northeastern Afghanistan it controlled: no more lifts for the growing back-log of khaki jackets wanting to hop the border.

It was the Dushanbe-Pyandzh rally two days later that saved us. That Friday was the day Dushanbe's traffic jams raced south to the border; the day its taxi-commuting public must have gone on foot; the day its taxi drivers got stinking rich with media dollars. Thirty taxis bearing a hundred hacks roared to the starting line outside the Tajik foreign affairs ministry, where officials had spent a day or more securing the necessary permissions for a land crossing from other government departments, from the Russians who controlled the border area by agreement with the Tajiks, and from the Afghans. Anything to get the clamouring hacks off their backs.

There was a final admonishment from a ministry official — follow the van in front bearing the official passes, stay together and wait for anyone who falls behind — and off we raced: the Charge of the Spotlight Brigade. Out of city limits the overtaking began. Along bumpy, potholed, narrow roads. Around blind bends in impossible mountain passes. In the face of oncoming traffic that veered at the last second.

Jamshed, the driver of the taxi that two SABC staffers (the only other South Africans) and I shared, was fast. After each stop he blindly clawed his way up the ranks until we were near the front of the convoy. Like many of his colleagues he drove an ancient Volga, the Mercedes of the Soviet Empire, although in appearance more akin to a Valiant. Jamshed, we decided, was the chairperson of the local Volga Solidarity Association. Whenever another Volga burst a tyre or developed mechanical problems, which was often, Jamshed stopped to help.

Jamshed's chairmanship almost cost us dearly. After one particularly time-consuming Volga breakdown session, during which the non-Volgas and some Volga defectors pressed on, we came to a checkpoint in a town appropriately named Moscowski, manned by the Russian FSB, successor to the KGB. The officers on duty demanded to see our passes, which we couldn't show because they were in the lead van that had long passed. It didn't help when a Spanish TV reporter bitched at an officer: "Didn't you know the KGB was disbanded in 1991?" His reply: "Really?"

Two hours of negotiations and phone calls later they let us go. Off roared the Volgas, save ours and two others. Volga number one's driver was missing. Volga number two screeched off to find him, only to splutter to a halt occasioned by mechanical failure that had no remedy. Volga number three — we — waited, Jamshed ever mindful of his duties as chair.

After dark Volga one and three, now labouring under the added weight of the occupants and luggage of Volga two, reached the final Russian checkpoint just short of the Pyandzh ferry. There, mercifully, the rest of the convoy was waiting for us, although about to leave. The South African contingent was last in the stable, but we had made it. In absolute darkness — we continued without lights due to the proximity of the Taliban, said to hold positions two or three kilometres beyond the river — 29 cars crawled down to the ferry.

But before we enter Afghanistan I owe the reader a glimpse of the land we had just traversed. Out of Dushanbe we entered a dusty countryside of rugged mountainous beauty and extreme deprivation. Tajikistan is the poorest of the former Soviet republics in Central Asia, still showing the scars of a five-year civil war that came to a fragile end in 1997. Up to 50 000 lives were lost in an orgy of clan fighting and ethnic cleansing. Tajikistan still struggles to cope with perhaps half a million internal refugees and twice as many people — almost one-sixth of the population — threatened by starvation.

I could not take my eyes off the people we passed in our hurry. Small and sturdy, they were beautiful, their majestic features carved finely on smooth olive skins. Men wore loose pants covered with tunics and waistcoats, often crowned by a turban or embroidered cap. Women shone in bright velvet and cotton dresses; symbolic veils loosely draped adding colour. And they all wore what seemed like a permanent air of bemusement, a refusal to capitulate to their lot.

But it was not these people or their circumstances the media convoy had come for. We pressed on to take our ringside seats in the US's "war on terrorism". I assuage my guilt with the rationalisation that the historical accident of border demarcation means the people south of the Pyandzh are yet to experience much more hardship than those we abandoned north.

Khwaja-Bahawudin is a time machine in fast reverse. A biblical scene decorated our first Afghan morning. A dusty sky blended with a maze of dust streets, high mud walls and flat mud dwellings. Bearded men, the same we saw north of the Pyandzh but with life etched more deeply into hardened faces, sauntered or led their mules. Women were invisible under their cover-all burkas if they ventured on the streets at all. Giggly children, the only colour on the streets, gawked at us. This town could have been there since the start of time and never changed (a few clanging jeeps, bakkies and trucks apart).

Khwaja-Bahawudin appeared on no map we saw. The town in its present form was too new — some three years old it was said. And that is when one realises that Afghanistan, or at least the territory that now goes by that name, is ancient. It cannot reproduce itself, spawn a new village or town, in ways recognisable to the modern eye.

Afghanistan is no state, either, as understood by the modern mind. To quote Jason Elliot in An Unexpected Light, an account of his travels in Afghanistan: "Yet there was a deeper obstacle to discovering the place: Afghanistan did not really exist. It was, more accurately, a fractured jewel, yielding a spectrum as broad or narrow as the onlooker's gaze ... It had never been a single country but a historically improbable amalgam of races and cultures, each with its own treasuries of custom, languages and visions of the world; its own saints, heroes and outlaws; an impossible place to understand as a whole."

Persian, Indian, Greek, Roman, Slavic, Mongol, Arab and Turkic blood courses through the Afghan veins. Each new invader of old — Genghis Khan, Alexander the Great and Tamberlane, among the more celebrated, each desirous of a foothold at the crossroads of Asia — left his progeny. In more recent times Tsarist Russia, the British Empire and the Soviet Union have tried their luck but left with little more than a fleeting contribution in blood (whether spilled or contributed to the ethnic mix) and a greater resolve on the part of an otherwise fractured Afghanistan to resist intrusion.

But back to Khwaja-Bahawudin: its importance, and its value to our collective media gaze, lay in the fact that Ahmed Shah Massood had set up military headquarters there in the last years of his life. Massood was preeminent among the mujahedin who fought the Soviets after their 1979 invasion. The Soviets retreated a decade later and when the mujahedin defeated their Afghan puppet, President Najibullah, in 1992, Massood rode victorious on his tank into the capital Kabul to become defence minister and supreme military commander.

But things fell apart. Infighting racked the new government led by President Barhuddin Rabbani, Massood and their Jamiat-e-Islami party. More factions persisted knocking at the doors of Kabul with heavy artillery. The city was ready for a fall, which it did to the Taliban in 1996. Massood retreated to the forbidding Panjshir Valley, his stronghold during the anti-Soviet struggle, and further north to Khwaja-Bahawudin. Under the largely symbolic leadership of Rabbani, Massood patched together the Northern Alliance, the main armed opposition to the Taliban.

My bed of concrete corridor (for space at the compound was limited) was a bed adjoining fate. I studied the ceiling darkened by soot, a wall on one side dangerously cracked, the plaster on the opposite wall marked as if by flying shards. What had been a door to an adjoining room was a broken hole, boarded up to keep the curious at bay.

Beyond that door was where Massood, age 49, took the shrapnel that ended his life. It happened on September 9. Two bogus journalists, said to be from Algeria, exploded their television camera in his face, sacrificing their own lives. The Alliance blamed Bin Laden and the Taliban. The latter probably blamed it on Alliance infighting. The timing was curious.

The rest was history: two days later the attacks on the US. A superpower baying for blood. Bin Laden and the Taliban blamed and condemned. War talk. Aid from Russia, the US and others pouring to the Alliance, giving it a first chance to change its stalemate with the Taliban. I had a job to do: the front line, my microscopic view of a war that may yet change the world.

On October 7 the SABC crew and I set off for the front line. We didn't get there. We queued an hour and more to get permission from Zubeir and his colleagues at the ministry. We bumped another hour along dusty roads to get to the headquarters of a General Mahebullah, front commander. His assistant waved us off, saying too many journalists were on that tour already; we'd have to come another day. More despondent hacks lounged about Mahebullah's courtyard, bitching about the unreliability of this "tourist agency".

The consolation prize was a tour to Koukcha river, a defensive line a few kilometres short of the front. Under the glare of dug-in tanks and machine gun posts we found, on the riverbank, an encampment that our translator, a young man with the beautiful name Baryolai Wazeen, called a "refugee hotel". Here, Baryolai said, refugees stopped en route from Taliban territory. Clay dung stoves supplied heat for tea and meals. A volleyball net was strung aside. No one played.

And it is there that I thought I could learn something of Afghanistan — but not in the guns that rumbled now and again in the background and not in the chapters of its disjointed and bloody history. I kidded myself, in that surreal landscape of desert dissected by fast-flowing river, that the faces of the people would reveal more. I stared at a leathery, bearded, turbaned face, which responded blankly. I peered at the fresh faces of the kids stoking fire. Unyieldingly they peered back. I chose the wide eyes of one little girl, who gigglily dug into my strange features as I into the innocence I thought I would find. She remained my enigma girl. My Afghanistan.

Events soon after revealed little more. The Northern Alliance was publicly encouraged by the US after September 11. It was waiting for the US-led attack on the Taliban to begin, to exploit the new situation to its own ends. But when news reached us that same evening that the bombing of Kabul and more targets had started, and when all crowded around the sole television set at the compound, there was no jubilation, no prediction of imminent victory — in fact no Alliance comment at all.

The sole quotes I could get that evening were from two Afghans at the compound, who bemoaned the fate of their country, the capital that was in the hands of their enemy, and their kin. Said one: "This [the bombing] is wrong. This is our city. I'm from Kabul. My wife, my children are there."

Two days later we made it to the front. Already before we arrived at the Koukcha our jeep was surrounded by men on horseback. They wanted $20 a horse for a few hours (about the price to buy a donkey) to take us through the river and beyond. I was a tourist again, elated on my grey stallion. And then we reached our front line, a barren hill of trenches facing the Taliban a hill beyond, mercifully shrouded in a cloud of dust. Two things happened there. First the avuncular commander who was our guide, Abdul Qudoos, insisted the US was no ally to him: "The Americans fight for revenge. We fight our fight that we have been fighting for seven or eight years."

Qudoos steadfastly refused to acknowledge his enemy's enemy as his friend. But then, just as a piece of the puzzle — Afghani pride and resentment at foreign interference — seemed to fall into place, he added: "If America attacks Afghanistan like last night and the night before, there will be no benefit for us, the people of Afghanistan. They should be more serious about it [presumably the bombing]."

The second thing that happened was that when one of the young soldiers in the trenches saw our cameras, he started firing into the distance for show. I saw bullets bite into the dust well short of the Taliban hill, but I pray none found a target. This was not my war. But it was a media war, and that included me. When another group of journalists hurried up the hill to "our" piece of the front, the same performance was repeated. And in the days that followed we heard story upon story how journalists, eager to show action, cajoled and bribed soldiers to exercise even heavy artillery, to make war for audiences back home. The theatre of war.

In my time that remained in Khwaja-Bahawudin I did the rest of the media tour: refugee camps. It was a topic worth the collective media gaze, with drought and displacement pushing seven and a half million people to the absolute brink.

At one such "camp" just outside town the seething mass of destitute did not live in tents or under plastic sheets as elsewhere. They were in the mud ruins of a settlement clearly inhabited by others before. I pressed the refugees, mostly ethnic Tajiks and Uzbeks pushed out by the Pashtun-dominated Taliban, on the identity of their predecessors. One relented: these houses used to belong to Pashtun who now, presumably, were refugees in Taliban territory. Not the standard story.

I bumped into a soft-spoken German, one of the few aid workers who had not deserted Afghanistan in anticipation of the US-led air strikes. Eric Engel told me the angels and the devils in this part of the world were not easy to distinguish. He feared the effects of the war on the suffering people and the power vacuum likely to follow the fall of the Taliban. "In the media the Talibs are presented as bad guys and the Northern Alliance as the good guys. That is a very simple view... The [Taliban] oppression is bad, but they also brought some peace and order, which Afghanistan did not have before."

As I write this the Taliban are already claiming 1 000 civilian deaths, the direct result of the US-led "war on terror". Numbers may be disputed, but in the weeks or months to come that figure will certainly surpass the casualties of the terror attacks on the US. And many, many times more in Afghanistan will succumb to their frailties induced by war. I see no outcome. Same old shit.

I cannot claim to understand Afghanistan or the forces, including the media, that moved the world's remaining superpower to want to pulverise a country of dust. But as certainly as Siamese drivers exist in Afghanistan, the small things I saw make sense. Life continues.

October 26 2001